A Single Thought

A Single Thought

by
Allen Hadidian

MOODY PRESS
CHICAGO

Library of Congress Cataloging in Publication Data

Hadidian, Allen, 1950-
  A single thought.

  Includes bibliographical references.
  1. Single people—Religious life. 2. Single
people in the Bible. I. Title.
BV4596.S5H32   248.8′4   81-38347
ISBN 0-8024-0878-8   AACR2

Second Printing, 1981

Printed in the United States of America

CONTENTS

This book is dedicated to John MacArthur and the college department of Grace Community Church. Over the past nine years my Christian life has been greatly enriched through their love, encouragement, and support.

FOREWORD

Unquestionably, the single person represents one of the most dynamic forces for effecting a spiritual change in this world. The single person is able to seek God and serve Him completely without distraction or encumbrance. As the apostle Paul points out, there is the potential for "undistracted devotion to the Lord" (1 Corinthians 7:35).

However, with these joys, many single Christians are painfully aware of their lack of a mate. They affirm that it is "not good for man to be alone" and yet realize that they are very much alone. In a day when there is an abundance of books written relating to marriage and the Christian family, it is encouraging to know that the needs of the single person have not been ignored but faced head on in *A Single Thought*.

Those struggling with the frustrations of singleness will be encouraged and strengthened. Those who are content will be motivated and challenged toward a greater appreciation of the freedoms and opportunities that a single life-style affords.

As a single person for the first thirty-one years of my life, I view the principles in *A Single Thought* as very relevant and needed in the Body of Christ. The content is highly personal and biblically based. I consider Allen's contribution in this area to be most credible in light of his personal experience, his previous ministry as a staff member for Campus Crusade for Christ, and his present ministry as college pastor of Grace Community Church.

Whether you are a content or frustrated single person, a leader of a singles ministry, or simply someone desirous of gaining insights into the single life-style, you will find *A Single Thought* to be a helpful companion. Your understanding of the needs, pressures, and desires of those who have not married will be deepened as a result of reading Allen's book.

JOSH MCDOWELL

ACKNOWLEDGMENT

I am deeply grateful to Susan Berger for her hours of labor in typing the manuscript.

PART I

The Bliss of the Single Life

INTRODUCTION

A reader might very well ask, "*Why* a book on the single life?"

I am single. I pastor a college-age group of several hundred single people. I have found that the average college-age person struggles with two major questions in his or her life. First, What am I going to do for the rest of my life? Second, With whom, if anyone, am I going to be doing it? Profession and marriage. Of the two, marriage represents the greatest tension and difficulty. How should one view his single state? How can one cope with his single state?

I have known the bliss, joys, and blessings that accompany the single life. I have also known the blisters—the hurts, frustrations, and struggles that accompany the single state.

I remember having been content in my singleness. I had no strong desires for marriage and no desire to date. My purpose was to do God's will, which I believed included studying the Word of God, discipling individuals, and having communion with God. I could not understand all the tensions of frustrated singles. I could not relate. Why would a person want to marry when time could be given to knowing the God of the universe and having communion with Him?

In fact, I remember that on one occasion I was so naive about the tensions that college-age people have regarding their desire for marriage that I acted very unwisely. I was leading singing in the college group on Sunday morning, and I decided to do a solo. I chose a song I had written for two very special people. There was nothing wrong with that—except that it was a wedding song. After I had sung, all the girls were in tears, and I walked away saying, "Oops."

I remember telling the Lord that He would have to work on my desires if He wanted me married. God began to work. The desire came, but along with the desire came many pressures. For the first time I had to deal with the problems of the single life. There was the pressure of friends' becoming engaged and getting married. Have you participated in many weddings? I have performed over twenty. I have had about every part you can have in a wedding. I have ushered, been the best man, sung a solo, and performed the ceremony.

I know what it is like to wake up every day with the reality of being single and the hurt that can easily go along with that. I know what it is like to receive invitations to weddings and hoping that I will be out of town that day. I know what it is like to go to bed at night wanting to put my arms around someone, but to have no one there.

I know what it is like to be lonely. I know what it is like to desire to love and be loved in an intimate way. I know all these things and many more. I also know what it is like to be ministered to and comforted by God. The book that follows contains principles and truths God has used to build me up.

I realize that the different people who are reading this book approach the subject of the single life with varying emotions. Some have always been glad that they are single. Others have always been angry that they are single. Some were glad at one point in their lives, but now they are mad. Some were mad in the past that they were single, but now they are glad. Some are content. Some are not able to handle their situation. Some are angry at God, others are just patiently waiting. The tensions felt are so different. Therefore God's solution will be unique and different. Some will need words of comfort. They will need to know that God is alive and well and loves them; that He is good, wise, and in control. Some will need words of conviction and confrontation.

I am glad that the Holy Spirit conveys truth to you and me. He will apply in each of our lives that which we need to know. I trust that there will be humility present in our lives that we might receive the truths from the Word of God. Often the truth we think does not apply may be the very truth the Holy Spirit uses to change us.

It is easy for single people to lose perspective about who they are, what God wants them to become, and what they are to be doing in the meantime. They struggle with that because they are attacked and pressured by the world in so many ways. Some desire to remain single but feel intimidated by the pressures of others to pursue marriage.

It is easy to lose one's perspective when one no longer thinks that the chief end of man is to glorify God and enjoy Him forever, but that it is to get married and have children forever.

How often have you heard that as a single person you are incomplete. One gets the idea that single people are valued at 25 percent of their worth until marriage. Then, all of a sudden, at 100 percent. Isn't it *amazing* how complete a person becomes when married! The Bible never says that man is 50 percent and the woman is 50 percent and when married they become 100 percent. Rather, man is 100 percent, woman is 100 percent and when they come together they make 200 percent.[1]

Singles are told that the three great goals of a person's life are master, mission, and mate. They often think that they have not made it until they have reached all three goals. Have you ever thought that you are a second-rate person because you are single?

"You are missing out." That statement by "well-meaning" friends makes one think he is missing out on God's wonderful plan because he is single.

Someone has said, "The plan of the Creator is marriage, not singleness . . . the plan of God is marriage. Singleness for religious service is a cultural tradition and not the plan of God."[2]

It is true that marriage is the norm, but marriage is not the plan for everyone. Some people are content to be single and have no desire for marriage. They are quite content, but there is real pressure put on them.

Those experiencing the bliss of married life often exhibit an air of superiority that makes singles believe they are second-class citizens. How many times have single people heard these words from their married friends: "Marriage is great! There's nothing like it! I would never want to be single again." That is as painful for some singles to hear as it is for a dying cancer victim to hear someone in his presence proclaim the bliss of health.

The comic strip writer, Tom K. Ryan, depicts this clearly in one of his scenes in *Tumbleweeds*. He shows a married woman telling a young single man, "Relax! I promise I won't even mention marriage . . . and its many blessings . . . as opposed to the creeping dry rot of bachelorhood.''[3] Sooner or later the criticism comes out, and the hurts intensify.

There is pressure from the church. Many of its activities are geared to the family. Singles are looked upon as if they do not belong.

There is pressure from the world. If you are nineteen or twenty and single, fine. If you are twenty to twenty-five you are told to ''Come on! Get with it!'' But if you are over twenty-five you hear, ''What is wrong with you?''

It is inevitable that one reasons this way: *Marriage is the norm. I am not married. Therefore, I am abnormal.* Have you ever felt that way?

We are pressured by age. One girl said regarding her singleness, ''I am getting so old! I cannot handle it! What am I going to do?''

''How old are you?''

''Eighteen.''

People pressure singles with questions. In fact, one becomes adept at answering such questions. One young lady was asked, ''Why aren't you married?''

''Oh,'' she said, ''I'm getting married on the first.''

''Wonderful! The first of what?''

''The first chance I get.''

Here are some pressuring statements and questions all singles face: ''Why aren't you married?'' ''Now remember, you are not getting any younger.'' ''Maybe you are a little bit too picky.'' ''Why is it that someone like you is not married?'' One single man was told, ''I don't understand. Something must be wrong with you. You should have been married a long time ago.'' Another was asked by a very concerned friend, ''I want you to level with me. Are you a homosexual?''

Unique pressure is placed on the single young man. A good friend of mine had a tremendous ministry with college-age people in another church, but the leaders wanted to find someone who was married. He was asked to leave, because he was not "qualified." Why? He was *single*.

There is family pressure. It is common to see parents pushing their children into marriage. They think, *We have to find you the right kind of person.* They force the issue and what happens? Some marriages turn out to be disastrous as the result of the prodding and the pushing of the parents, rather than coming about in the design of the will of God. If you are single and live at home you may face another form of parental pressure. Imagine this happening . . .

"Son, have you thought about marriage?"

"Well, I don't know, Dad. I guess I have thought about it."

"Well, we do not want to put any pressure on you, but your mother and I are seriously talking about turning your bedroom into a den!"

That is a bit extreme, yet some singles sense that attitude even though it may not be said.

Pressure is produced by believing that one will not get married until he becomes the right kind of person. There may be *some* truth to that statement, but it becomes so easy to start thinking that marriage is reserved for the spiritual ones.

Singles have not found much encouragement in Christian books. Few meaningful books are written on the single person, though many on marriage and the family.

With all these pressures, it is not surprising that many women find themselves echoing the sentiments expressed in this poem. It is entitled "The Unknown Man."

Oh, unknown man, whose rib I am,
why don't you come for me?
A lonely, homesick rib I am
that would with others be.
I want to wed—there, now, 'tis said!
(I won't deny and fib.)
I want my man to come at once
and claim his rib!

Some men have thought that I'd be
theirs, but only for a bit;
We found out soon it wouldn't do—
we didn't seem to fit.
There's just one place, the only space
I'll fit (I will not fib).
I want that man to come at once
and claim his rib!

Oh, don't you sometimes feel a lack,
a new rib needed there?
It's I! Do come and get me soon before
I have gray hair.
Come get me, dear! I'm homesick here!
I want (and I'll not fib).
I want my man to come at once
And claim his rib*
                Judy Downs Douglass, "The Unknown Man"

Another individual expresses it this way:

Our culture reinforces such feelings in a thousand ways. Our
whole society is couple-oriented. Parents expect their children

*Printed by permission. Copyright © Here's Life Publishers,
Inc. All rights reserved.

to marry; so do their friends and relatives, and society at large. There are sexual tensions and strong peer pressures. Despite today's changing attitudes towards marriage, the person who marries late or not at all is considered an oddity, not quite normal. Sexual aberrations may be suspected, even hinted at. People feel free to question, to tease, to make sick jokes about singleness as they would dare to do about no other personal matter. The world pairs off and the single is left out of its activities. She no longer fits in at all; he, though he may still be welcome, soon finds he no longer really belongs. Though things are easier for singles today than ever before, there isn't a single alive who has not suffered under some of these pressures. The single woman may have to live with the shattering knowledge that no one has ever desired her; the single man with the bitter fact that he has been rejected.[4]

How is one to view his single state? How should one respond to it? Does God want him to view it as nothing more than a "social purgatory"? The only ray of hope may be the possibility of some day being released, but haunting and horrifying is the possibility that the single life may be life imprisonment! Is *that* how God wants a person to view his singleness?

1

Freedom in Single Living

No chapter in the Bible more completely examines the topic of the bliss of the single life than 1 Corinthians 7. This chapter contains the most definitive statement that God has made on the single life. Paul begins in verse 1 by saying, "Now concerning the things about which you write, it is good for a man not to touch a woman." "To touch" literally means "to take hold of." This concept of touching a woman or taking hold of a woman, a euphemism for sexual intercourse, is used by the Greek writer Xenophon to denote marriage.

In Genesis 20:4-6 and Genesis 26:10-11, there are potential cases where adultery could have been committed in the family of Abraham, but God did not let Abimelech "touch" Abraham's wife or Isaac's wife. "To touch" means to have physical relationships. The same concept is seen in Ruth 2:9. Boaz had a desire to keep Ruth pure and therefore commanded the men not to touch her. Proverbs 6:29 says, "So is the one who goes in to his neighbor's wife; whoever touches her will not go unpunished."

Paul says that it is good not to have sexual relationships. It is good to be single. It is OK for a man not to marry.

However, it is important to understand that Paul is not saying that the single state is the *only* good. Paul recognizes that it is good to be married. He is simply saying that it is not evil to be single. He does not say that you will sin if you marry. Verse 28 says, "But if you should marry, you have not sinned; and if a virgin should marry, she has not sinned."

Paul does not say it is morally right only to be single. He does not say that being single is the only right thing to do. He says it is *kalas,* or fair, or beneficial, or profitable. He is stating a fact, not comparing the unmarried condition with the married condition. He is simply confirming that singlehood is OK. So right away Paul's statement destroys all the pressures one feels and all the exhortations one fears emphasizing the need to get married—pressures stemming from the suggestion that if you are not married and if you have no desire to get married, there is something wrong with you.

Paul then says in verse 6, "But this I say by way of concession, not of command." Literally, "I keep on saying this." The verb is in the present tense, and this refers to the single status. What Paul is about to say has to do with those who were still single. We know this from the conjunction "but" in verse 6. It sets up a contrast with what he said in verses 1-5 regarding marriage. What he is saying is that the principle of single status in verse 7 is not a command for all believers. He says this in verse 7, "Yet I wish that all men were even as I myself am." He does not command that for all believers. He does not command them to be single. He says, "Yet I wish that all men were even as I myself am, that is, single." Then he repeats the same idea in verse 8. "But I say to the unmarried and to widows that it is good for them if they remain even as I.'' It is good to be single. If you are a bachelor, that is good. If you are a single young girl, that is good. If you are a maiden who has never been married, Paul says that is good. If you are a widow or widower, that is good. It is obvious that Paul's purpose is to be single. He is not looking for a wife, and he will not look for a wife. You ask, ''Why? What's wrong with him? Doesn't he know that marriage is great? How can Paul make such a statement? Why does he say that he wishes that everyone was as he was—single? Why should he personally desire that all believers be single?'' That takes us to verses 25-35.

Possibly at this point you are thinking, ''Do not think you can pass over verse 9 so quickly.'' Do not worry; we will examine that in a later chapter. In fact, the apostle's exhortations in verses 25-35 are to be heeded only if one does not have this so-called ''gift of celibacy.'' But even though a person may get married in the future there are principles and truths that God wants us to know right now. He wants us to understand these things concerning single life regardless of whether we have the ''gift of celibacy.'' God is saying, ''I have things for you to understand now in your singleness. I have principles I want you to consider.''

In verses 25-35 we are going to examine three reasons for remaining single, reasons the apostle believes the single state to be good. The world says that singles are incomplete. The world says that singles are missing out. The world says that singles are to be left out. The world says singles do not belong. Pauls says, ''It is good to be single.'' Let us find out why.

Since we will be examining this chapter, we need to understand several points by way of background. First, at the time of the writing of 1 Corinthians, Paul was single, though probably married at one time. Two points support this. First, Jewish boys married at the age of eighteen in Bible days. The Mishnah fixed the age of marriage at seventeen or eighteen, and the Babylonian Jews set the age as early as fourteen. Marriage was regarded as a duty among the Jews, so that a man was considered to have sinned if he had reached the age of twenty without marrying. In fact, a single man past twenty years of age could be compelled by the court to marry. One writer states, "He who is without a wife is without joy, without blessing, without happiness, without learning, without protection, without peace; indeed he is no man; for it is written (Genesis 5:2), 'Male and female created He them, and called their name man.' "[5] "He who is not married is, as it were, guilty of blood shed and deserves death. He causes the image of God to be diminished and the divine presence to withdraw from Israel."[6]

There was a belief that being single lessened the image of God and man. How? It meant that you were incapable of being fruitful and multiplying. You had to be married, or you would violate God's command to replenish the earth. A man who did not have a wife and a child had slain his posterity, and he lessened the image of God in this world. So to be a good Hebrew demanded that you take a wife and have children.

In fact, to show you the extent to which they went, the Jews had a list of the seven kinds of persons who were unacceptable to God. Number one was a Jew who had no wife, and number two was a Jewish person who had no children.

Another convincing argument that Paul was married at one point was that he was a member of the Sanhedrin, according to Acts, chapters 8 and 26. Every member had to be married. So

Paul was single at the time of the writing of 1 Corinthians, though married once.

Second, Paul is not dealing here with the subject of marriage in general, but he is answering direct questions that the Corinthians had previously addressed to him. He says in verse 1 of chapter 7, "Now concerning the things about which you wrote . . ." The Corinthians had written Paul a letter, probably carried to him by the people mentioned in 16:17—Stephanas, Fortunatus, and Achaicus. The Corinthians had many problems, and we do not know exactly what those problems were, or what those direct questions were, but by Paul's answers we are given a clue as to what the issues were. They did not know whether marriage was a necessary part of spirituality or not. Some were saying a truly devoted Christian would not marry. The Jews were saying that if you are a devoted Christian you will get married.

Regardless of the issues involved, Paul is not dealing with the subject of marriage in general. No attempt is made to state the Christian doctrine of marriage in its fullness. To get that, one needs to look at Ephesians or Colossians.

Paul is answering some direct questions in 1 Corinthians 7. That needs to be understood, or else one might think that Paul regards marriage as a lower state than single living. But that is not true; that is not Paul's perspective. In fact, he himself said in 1 Timothy 4 that the teaching that marriage is forbidden is a doctrine of demons.

Third, the instructions Paul gives in this chapter were in light of special conditions existing at that time and place. In verse 26 he says, "This is good for the present distress." When Paul wrote 1 Corinthians, his whole outlook was dominated by the fact that he expected Christ to return soon. Therefore, Paul writes to the Corinthians as he would to an army about to enter an enemy's territory. He tells them that this is not the time for them to think about marriage. They have a right to marry, and marriage is the norm, but in their circumstances, marriage can only lead to problems. Even though this is the historical context, Paul's teachings are based on great underlying principles that are always true. The principles he shares are general regardless of the historical context.

With that as a background, let us consider verses 25-35.

> Now concerning virgins I have no command of the Lord, but I give an opinion as one who by the mercy of the Lord is trustworthy. I think then that this is good in view of the present distress, that it is good for a man to remain as he is. Are you bound to a wife? Do not seek to be released. Are you released from a wife? Do not seek a wife. But if you should marry, you have not sinned; and if a virgin should marry, she has not sinned. Yet such will have trouble in this life, and I am trying to spare you. But this I say, brethren, the time has been shortened, so that from now on those who have wives should be as though they had none; and those who weep, as though they did not weep; and those who rejoice, as though they did not rejoice; and those who buy, as though they did not possess; and those who use the world, as though they did not make full use of it; for the form of this world is passing away. But I want you to be free from concern. One who is unmarried is concerned about the things of the Lord, how he may please the Lord; but one who is married is concerned about the things of the world, how he may please his wife, and his interests are divided. And the woman who is unmarried, and the virgin, is concerned about the things of the Lord, that she may be holy both in body and spirit; but one who is married is concerned about the things of the world, how she may please her hus-

band. And this I say for your own benefit; not to put a restraint upon you, but to promote what is seemly, and to secure undistracted devotion to the Lord.

Paul writes in verse 25: "Now concerning virgins . . ." That word "virgins" is *parthenoi,* and it simply means one who is unmarried, or in single status. God equates virginity with singleness, and here the feminine article is used, so it refers to unmarried women. But this passage deals with both men and women because in verse 26 he says that it is good for a man to remain as he is. He uses the word *anthropos,* or man.

Paul says, "Concerning virgins, I have no command of the Lord, but I give an opinion." What does that mean? The Lord spoke on many topics when He was on earth. When Paul was saying something the Lord had said, he acknowledged that. In verse 10, he says, "But to the married I give instructions, not I, but the Lord." In other words, the Lord said something specifically on that topic. But when the Lord did not talk on it, Paul gives his opinion.

It is interesting that the Lord Jesus had much to say concerning marriage and divorce but very little to say about the concept of being single. John 16:12-13 says that there are many things that the Lord Jesus Christ did not cover but that would be included later by the apostles. He would reveal truths to them. Although the Lord did not cover the subject, the Holy Spirit is directing Paul to declare these things. Paul is giving his authoritative, inspired opinion. It is the good advice of the Holy Spirit through him. Paul cannot command that everyone be single, because God has never commanded that. God says that the norm is marriage, so when Paul speaks on the single life he is in the realm of inspired opinion, not commands.

What he is about to say is not a binding law, because some will not remain single.

In verse 25 Paul says that he gives his opinion as one who, by the mercy of the Lord, is trustworthy. It is not just the counsel of a wise man, but one who obtained mercy. He is believable and worthy of confidence. His judgment on this matter can be trusted.

2

Freedom from Pressure

First Corinthians 7:26-28 contains the first reason Paul gives us regarding the bliss of the single life. Single people have freedom from certain pressure. In verse 26 Paul says, "I think then that this is good." Literally, Paul means that he has an authoritative, inspired conviction about something. He continues, "I think then this is good in view of the present distress . . ." The idea of "present" can express something that actually is there now or something that is impending.

In the first century the church was just getting started, and there was tremendous satanic pressure. It was a time when Satan launched an all-out counter-offensive to hinder the operation of the church. It was a time of oppression. It was a time of persecution. Satan wanted to keep the first-century evangelists and ministers from evangelizing the world. In Paul's mind the presence of that persecution forshadowed and would inaugurate something to come—the coming of the Lord Jesus Christ.

The word *distress* means violence, calamity, or straits. In Luke 21:23 the word talks of the violence of the Great Tribula-

27

tion. John 15:18-20 and John 16:1-3 confirm the fact that the world will hate and persecute Christians. It is interesting to note that ten years after 1 Corinthians was written, persecution really broke out under Nero, the sixth emperor of Rome. Some Christians were sewed up in the skins of wild beasts and then turned over to dogs, who tore them to pieces. Others were dressed in garments that were made stiff with wax in order to be fixed to trees and then lit like candles to light his garden.

Paul saw all this coming, and it should be no surprise to Christians today as we face the same things. One sees immorality, persecution, revolution, disease, dictatorship, depression, and oppression. It is a very rough and distressing world in which we live. It is a world of calamity, especially for Christians, and until Jesus Christ returns we can expect hatred from the world.

Paul says that in light of this, it is good for a man to remain as he is. He says that since the present condition is indeed trying, there is no point to make any significant change in one's ordinary way of life. Verses 26-27 state: "It is good for a man to remain as he is. Are you bound to a wife? Do not seek to be released." Even though celibacy may be better in time of stress and pressures, seek not to be released from marriage either by divorce or separation. Do not try to get out of it. Then Paul further states in verse 27: "Are you released from a wife? Do not seek a wife." In other words, if a person is single now, Paul's advice is to remain single. If one is married, remain married. Do not let there be any significant change in the progression of your life.

Verse 28 gives the balance. "But if you should marry, you have not sinned; and if a virgin should marry, she has not sinned." A change in marital status is not wrong. There is nothing wrong in getting married. Paul is not against marriage because it is sinful. To Paul, it is permissible to marry; it just is not always advisable. Marriage may not be expedient, but also it is not sinful. Even though under certain circumstances or conditions it is better to remain in the single state, no one has sinned by getting married. Paul simply suggests that one consider the option of not marrying.

Calvin states: "In view of the 'difficulties' which always press hard upon the saints in this life, I think that the best solution is for all to enjoy the freedom and independence of celibacy, for it would be a real benefit to them." In other words, there are distressing things that believers constantly run up against in this distressing, calamity-filled world.

The reader may contend that he is still not convinced. Why should he consider the option of *not* marrying? Verse 28 supplies the answer: "Yet such will have trouble in this life, and I am trying to spare you." Paul says that he is giving these injunctions in order to spare them trouble in this life. What does "trouble in this life" mean? Literally it is "tribulation in the flesh." The word "trouble" is the Greek word *thlipsis*. It comes from a word meaning "to press together." It was used of the squashing or pressing of grapes together to extract the juice. That is *thlipsis*, or pressure. It is used in John 16:21 of the anguish or distress of a woman in childbirth. Matthew 24:21 speaks of the Great Tribulation, or the great pressure.

Paul prefers the single state over marriage, not for its own sake, but rather for what it leads to. He says that trouble or pressure are inseparable from married life. Marriage brings many troubles and pressures along with it, and he says that to spare us. In other words, he wants to encourage the Corinthians to adopt the single life-style that they may be lifted above the troubles that go along with marriage.

What Paul is saying seems to be inconsistent with what the Lord God said in Genesis 2:18: "It is not good for the man to be alone." In his work on 1 Corinthians 7 Calvin has said:

> . . . sin made its attack and spoiled that institution of God [marriage] for in place of so great a blessing grievous affliction (*poena*) has entered in, so that marriage is the source and means of many troubles. Therefore whatever evil or trouble there is in marriage springs from the corruption of God's institution. Although there is still something left of the original blessing, so that the life of a single person is often much more miserable than that of a married person, yet, in view of the fact that married people are involved in many misfortunes, Paul is justified in advising that it would be good for a man to keep from it. . . . What it amounts to is this, that we must remember to distinguish between the unblemished ordinance of God, and the punishments of sin, which came on the scene afterwards. For, according to this distinction, in the beginning it was good for a man to be joined to a wife, without anything to spoil it; and even now it is good but only to a degree, because the bitter is mixed with the sweet, on account of the curse of God.[1]

Calvin is saying that if we had a world without sin and people without sin Paul would not have raised that point at all. But the added dimension of sin brings pressure to a marriage. Paul is not saying that marriage is a necessary evil. The troubles of which he is speaking do not arise so much from marriage itself but rather from the way sin has corrupted it. Paul is not saying that all of marriage is one big pressure, but rather that pressures accompany marriage. Paul recommends the single state that we might be free from pressure.

In a marriage or family context there is a greater propensity for pressure than in a single context. When one looks at the tensions that exist between the new creation and the world, it is easy to see how marriage can complicate living because of the added responsibilities. There are less encumbrances in single living.

In marriage, during times of intense persecution, the man or woman would have to endure not only individual suffering, but also the pain and grief of seeing a husband, a wife, or a child suffer as well. It is easier for many to suffer themselves than to see their loved ones suffer. The nearer one gets to the end times, the higher the price he may have to pay for his faith. Paul says if a person is single it is easier to pay that price.

A man became the pastor of a small church. He had been there for three weeks when representatives of the neighborhood group came to him and told him not to teach on "certain issues." This man continued to preach the need to love God and one's neighbor. The community turned against that man. He would get phone calls in the middle of the night at ten-minute intervals with obscenities or silence at the other end. He would get in his car only to find the tires deflated. He would walk down the main street of the town, and people would spit on him. All this led him to tell his fiancée that marriage was out of the question, because he did not want to take her to live in a place like that. He knew the reality of persecution pressure.

In his book *Tortured for Christ,* Richard Wurmbrand says:

> A pastor by the name of Florescu was tortured with red-hot iron pokers and with knives. He was beaten very badly. Then starving rats were driven into his cell through a large pipe. He could not sleep, but had to defend himself all the time. If he rested a moment, the rats would attack him. He was forced to stand for two weeks, day and night. The communists wished to compel him to betray his brethren, but he resisted steadfastly.

> In the end, they brought his fourteen-year-old son and began to whip the boy in front of his father, saying that they would continue to beat him until the pastor said what they wished him to say. The poor man was half mad. He bore it as long as he could. When he could not stand it any more, he cried to his son, "Alexander, I must say what they want! I can't bear your beating any more!"[2]

That is persecution pressure.

I had never truly considered this point as an advantage of being single. I had to stop and think, *If the United States ever got to a point where physical persecution was a reality because of religious beliefs, would I pursue marriage? I would probably wait it out.*

Put yourself in the shoes of a young, single Ugandan Christian in the 1970s. Imagine seeing thousands of your Christian brothers and sisters killed because they named the name of Christ. Imagine hearing countless stories of how Idi Amin's secret police would unexpectedly come and take a husband away from his wife or a wife away from her husband. Imagine seeing your own mother grief-stricken as your father was arrested and executed because he was a Christian. I would seriously consider Paul's advice.

For the single person there is freedom from this persecution pressure. No one is dependent upon us. We do not have the responsibility to care for someone, so we do not feel the pressure that those who are married feel. We are more expendable. That is a hard way to put it. We are front line troops to confront the world, and we really cannot be affected by the death or separation of a wife or a husband or a child.

Think of Paul's ministry in this regard. There was definite wisdom in his being single. Look at his ministry. He would go into a town, and they would put him in jail. He would go into another town, and they would beat him. He would enter a third town, and they would stone him. He experienced the "present distress" in an intense way. He was spared from trouble in the flesh by being single. In what way?

Imagine the weight on Paul's mind had he been married, thinking of his wife at home and all the children. That would have been pressure, an added weight. *Who will take care of my wife if something happens to me? What about the children?* That is persecution pressure, and single living brings some relief from that kind of pressure.

There is another kind of pressure felt within marriage, and it is caused by the sin natures of the husband and the wife. Single life avoids this kind of pressure. I call it "freedom from humanness" pressure. I am told that one quickly realizes something in marriage. You realize that the husband is a sinner, and you realize that the wife is a sinner. Do you know what happens when you put two sinners together? *Thlipsis*—pressure. Then children come, more sinners come into being, and that is what I call the complete household—totally depraved. It is the humanness in marriage that makes for trouble.

Marriage is a pressing together, and there is the trouble that pressing together brings. Think of two or more people living together, whether in a family or roommate situation. Whatever it might be, there will be anger that needs to be dealt with. There will be selfishness that needs to be dealt with. There will be pride that needs to be dealt with. Paul says that he is trying to spare them that. Paul gives them that information, not to make them miserable and unhappy or to frustrate them but to spare them difficulties along the way. He wants his readers to take an honest look at married life, because many single people think that marriage would solve all of their problems and relieve all their pressure.

One person has said: "Singles who feel themselves unfulfilled are usually convinced that marriage would solve all their problems. The grass is always greener on the other side of the fence. Once in a while it does no harm to take a long, sober look at what is actually growing in other pastures."[3] Paul says there is tribulation in the flesh. Marriage is not a cure-all to the ills of singleness. The problems one has as a single individual will be the problems one will take into marriage. Marriage does not change every problem; it just makes someone else share that problem with them.

Some think that marriage will bring a greater spirituality to their lives. They have the attitude: "I am doing well with the Lord, but if I were married, I would really be spiritual." How untrue! If you are spiritually weak now, then you will be spiritually weak in a marriage relationship. If you are a spiritually weak woman now, the chances are that, if married, you will be a spiritually weak wife. If you are a spiritually weak man, you will be a spiritually weak husband. Saying, "I do," does not change a thing. You will just take your spiritually weak condition into marriage, and that spells *thlipsis,* or pressure.

We must not think that marriage is a cure-all to our troubles, but we tend to do that. The most miserable people in the world are not troubled single people; the most miserable people in the world are those who are troubled and *married*. In fact, the only thing worse than waiting is wishing you had.

One man has said that it is better to go through life wanting what you do not have, rather than having what you do not want. Many people end up saying, "I do," to somebody, thinking that will make them something they are not before marriage, only to say after marriage that they would rather have remained single. Let us not think that marriage will end our troubles. Marriage is not the solution to our problems.

"But, Allen," you might be saying, "those are some strong statements. Does that mean that all marriages are destined to be like that?" *No!* You have to remember that something happened in Adam and Eve's relationship after they sinned against God, bringing tensions and pressures to the marriage relationship that did not exist previously. A marriage relationship has built into it the potential of much pressure and conflict. That makes Ephesians 5:18 so critical.

We are to be *filled* with the Holy Spirit. Why? When we are filled with the Holy Spirit, then we have the capacity and enablement to recapture what God intended a marriage relationship to be. I look at some marriage relationships where Christ is not the center, and I think to myself, *It is good to remain as I am: single.* Then I look at a marriage where Christ is the center; both husband and wife are walking by the Spirit, and there is a commitment to each other, a working together, and a deep joy. Then I think, *It is not good for man to be alone.* Do you get the point? Marriage between people who are not Spirit-filled can be disastrous. Marriage in which both the husband and wife are controlled and empowered by God's Spirit is a beautiful, meaningful reality.

3

Freedom to Serve

First Corinthians 7:29-31 reveals the second reason the single life is bliss—there is freedom to serve. He says, "This I say, the time has been shortened." In the original Greek there is no verb in the phrase "The time has been shortened." Literally it says, "The time, short." The word used for "time" is not *chronos* but another word. *Chronos* is time like a clock or a calendar. It is time like a sequence of minutes. We have chronology, or the flow of events, in history. We have a chronograph—something that keeps time. But the word here is *kairos*. It means the set time, the appointed time.

Specifically, Paul is talking about opportunities. He says the opportunities are shortened. What does the word *shorten* mean? It is an interesting word that means "to roll up, to wind up." The only other time it is used is in Acts 5:6, and there it refers to the winding up of Ananias. In classical Greek it was used in relation to packing luggage or reducing one's expenses. The idea of "shortened," therefore, is that of restriction. He is referring to opportunities to serve Christ and to further His kingdom.

He continues in verse 29: "The time has been shortened, so that from now on those who have wives should be as though they had none; and those who weep, as though they did not weep." What does that mean? That husbands should run around with other women and neglect their own wives? That husbands ought to mistreat their wives and not fulfill their obligations?

Verse 30 says we are to be as though we did not weep. In other words, should we be callously unconcerned at the grief of our friends? No! Paul mentions five legitimate activities that depict the lives of most Christians: marrying, sorrowing, rejoicing, possessing, and enjoying worldly pleasures. Paul is telling Christians that they should think a certain way toward marriage, toward sorrow, toward joy, toward possessions, and toward worldly pleasures.

What is the underlying reason? If time is short, if the opportunities are restricted, then there are all too few moments to live for Christ. It is Paul's perspective that nothing should stand in the way of whole-hearted commitment to Christ. The point Paul is making in verses 29-31 is that we must adopt a detached attitude toward all present earthly experiences. Paul desires that in light of the fact that opportunities are restricted, we should attach ourselves lightly to earthly things. It is his desire that none of these five activities come between us and the Lord. They must not completely occupy our time. We must hold earthly ties and possessions loosely. Why? To Paul the first order of business is eternity. Let us examine these five activities.

First, in verse 29, opportunities are restricted, so that "from now on both those who have wives should be as though they had none." He is talking here about marriage. We will touch on this briefly and then come back to it. While loving the husband or the wife, married individuals are not to forget that the opportunities are restricted. The time is short. In other words, make sure that marriage does not hinder the proper use of your time before the Lord.

Second, he says in verse 30: "And those who weep, as though they did not weep." This is not some kind of stoical precept: Refrain from weeping. Grief is human, but we are to weep remembering that the time is short and that opportunities are restricted. There are times we will weep, and it is hard to avoid that. In fact, Romans 12 says that we are to weep with those who weep.

But Paul says that we should not be improperly affected by passing events. Our grief should be moderated by the hope of a life to come and by that which is eternal. Paul is saying not to be overly affected by human emotion. Why? Because when we get to heaven God is going to wipe away every tear. Paul says to make sure that your weeping does not hinder the proper use of your time before the Lord. If the opportunities are restricted, we do not have the time to be consumed with grief. Paul says the opportunities are restricted; do not allow human emotion to keep you from that which needs to be done now.

Third, in verse 30, "And those who rejoice, as though they did not rejoice." Those who are happy, those who have prospered, those who have been blessed with success, with honor, who have had esteem, whatever the reason—those people should be as though they did not rejoice. Those people should not be satisfied with those things, even though they might rejoice in them. They should be as though they did not rejoice because any earthly happiness will soon go.

Christianity does not frown on earthly happiness. No one

should enjoy God's world like us, His children. But again, the tempering thought comes into focus. It is Paul's desire that in light of the fact that the opportunities are restricted, our rejoicing in earthly happiness should be moderated with the thought that there is more to living than that which is temporal. Again he is saying to make sure that your rejoicing does not hinder the proper use of your time before the Lord; do not be consumed with it.

Fourth, "And those who buy as though they did not possess." Here he is talking about the legitimate activity of buying. It is good to buy and possess things. Every lawful way of acquiring wealth and goods is open to us as Christians. We are not prohibited from acquiring possessions, but the question is, "What place do they have in our hearts?" We should have a conviction that these possessions will be left some day. All that we possess is temporal. We will possess them for a time, and then they will just pass into the hands of someone else.

Paul says that in light of the fact that the opportunities are restricted and possessions are temporal, we should live above the world and secure a treasure in the heavenly world where no thief approaches and where moths cannot corrupt. We are not to get overly preoccupied with the world's commodities. That is hard to do sometimes. It is easy to be more worried about our bank accounts than our spiritual lives. In our concern with making money and buying things Paul says to make sure that the activity of buying does not hinder the proper use of our time before the Lord because the opportunities are restricted.

Fifth, he says in verse 31, "And those who use the world as though they did not make full use of it." The word "use" refers to the lawful use of the world. We are to use the world, its food, its clothing, and its protection. But we are not to use it to excess. We are not to take our fill of its pursuits as our chief aim, as did the man in Luke who built all those barns in order to accommodate all his goods. We should be *in* the world but not *of* it. The spirit of the world says that time is short, so take your fill. The narrow religious spirit says: "All the pleasure here is a snare. It is dangerous. Keep out of it altogether. Do not get involved in it."

But in opposition to the narrow spirit Christianity says, "Use the world." In opposition to the worldly spirit, Christianity says, "Do not abuse it. All things are yours, take them and use them but never let them interfere with the higher life that you were called to lead." Again, it is so easy to fall into the thinking that we are to live simply to have a good time—to travel here, to vacation there, to relax.

Paul says that we are to give ourselves to those things that are going to have eternal consequences. Preoccupation with pleasure must not be our life-style. Paul tells us to make sure that the involvement in worldly pleasure does not hinder the proper use of our time before the Lord, because opportunities are restricted.

Why does he say all this about legitimate worldly activities? Verse 31: "For the form of this world is passing away." The figure here is derived from the scenes of a theater in the actual process of change. The shifting scenes of a play are what is depicted. When the scene changes, the pageantry passes. The fashion of the world is unreal and elusive. It changes. It continues for a little time, and then the scene changes. It vanishes. What is here today is gone tomorrow. Today the world is busy with one set of actors; tomorrow a new company appears, only to be succeeded by another. He says that if this is what the world is all about, how little we should set our affections upon it. We should be prepared for the real and unchanging scenes of another world. Our participation in this world's joys and sorrows are short-lived. We should not be wedded to earthly things.

We are not to value human relationships, emotions, possessions, or pleasures above their true worth. All the things that make for enriching life are gifts from God, but we spoil them by misusing them. We need to live as if we might have to leave this world at any moment. Paul wants us to use these things in a moderate and disciplined way so that we will not be hindered or delayed but that we will be pressing on toward the goal. According to Paul, who preferred the single life, marriage can be a hindrance that keeps us from pressing on toward that goal. Human emotions, possessions, and pleasures can hinder also.

Paul wants Christian single people to gain a perspective of Christian living and live with eternity in mind. He wants us to set our affections on things above (Colossians 3:2). He does not want us to be absorbed with the events of this life. Paul is saying, "Realize, Christians, that the opportunities are restricted, and the moments that can be grasped for God are restricted."

The Greeks had a statue named *Opportunity*. It was carved and chiseled by a man named Lysippas. It had wings on its feet, a great lock of hair in the front, and it was bald in back. Carved in Greek on the base of the statue was this dialogue:

> Who made thee?
> Lysippas made me.
> What is thy name?
> My name is Opportunity.
> Why hast thou wings on thy feet?

> That I may fly away swiftly.
> Why hast thou a forelock?
> That men may seize me when I come.
> Why art thou bald in back?
> When I am gone by, none can lay hold of me.[1]

The opportunities are restricted; the world is passing away. Grab those opportunities.

Ephesians 5:15-16 exhorts, "Therefore be careful how you walk, not as unwise men, but as wise, making the most of your time, because the days are evil." From Paul's perspective, if we are able to remain single, so much the better. He cannot command us to remain single, because marriage is the norm and he recognizes that.

As single people we need to ask God to give us a sense of urgency in the days that we live, that we might seize every opportunity. Paul feels that the single life would be a definite advantage when one considers the opportunities that are available. According to Paul, marriage is part of the passing form of this world. If a person has the "gift of singleness," then that part of the passing system is not needed.

Marriage can be such a preoccupation that one is not able to concentrate on the opportunities at hand. Marriage is a temporal, passing relationship. It demands a certain kind of attachment, and that attachment is not necessarily bad. But it takes time and energy to plan out certain things that go along with being married. For example, one must be concerned with buying life insurance, medical insurance, a house, saving money for children, being sensitive to the psychological, spiritual, and emotional needs of the family.

Who struggles with the lack of time—single people or married people? Is the tension greater in those who are married or those who are single? I believe those who are married struggle the most. Single people are usually dealing more in responsibilities with *things*, whereas married people have a tremendous sense of responsibility and accountability to the Lord for another *person;* that responsibility demands a certain commitment of time. Paul suggests that if a person has the gift of singleness he is better off to remain single.

You have to understand that Paul was consumed with the desire to serve the Lord. It was his desire to have all believers spend as much time as possible in the Lord's service. Paul recommends the single life, because singles have an unbelievable potential for buying up the opportunities to further God's kingdom.

When Paul was on his second missionary journey he came to Lystra and met Timothy. Paul wanted this man to go with him. Timothy, being single, had the time to go with Paul. If God calls a single person to a certain ministry, he has fewer factors to weigh than a married person. A single person's time can be used by more people than a select few.

Singles have more time than those who are married. (Some might argue that point, especially those singles who live away from home, have a work week of about forty hours, have to shop, go to school, clean, do the laundry, cook, and everything else.) They also have greater flexibility with their time. We are able to adjust our personal schedule to fit special needs when they arise unexpectedly. We are able to do that, because we have only our needs to consider and not those of a family. We have freedom to serve and to seize those opportunities.

One young man was telling me that he met someone at a home Bible study, and he wanted to meet with that person the next night because of the need in that person's life. Suddenly he realized that the next night was a time he had planned to spend with his fiancée. There was a tension within him. There is greater flexibility for single people.

I remember being with some brothers and expressing some personal needs and struggles in my own life. Two of them had to leave to get back to their wives, but the one who remained with me was single. I am not saying that the others were not concerned; they were. In fact, one of the married men who had to leave invited me to come home with him and have dinner with him and his family. There was concern, but I am saying that we single people have a tremendous freedom in the use and flexibility of our time.

Our evenings are very free. Some of you are thinking, *Oh, no, they are not! Why I have a discipling group on Monday, an evening service on Wednesday, visitation on Thursday, and a home Bible study on Friday. Why, my evenings are loaded!* I will agree they are filled, but *you* have the choice. That is the bliss of being single—we can fill up our schedules the way we want them filled. We can choose to get involved in a specific ministry, or we can choose not to get involved. It is our choice. We do not have to check with anyone.

We have freedom to disciple someone. We have freedom to visit someone when we want to. If I am asked to teach a Bible class on a certain evening, I do not have to be concerned that I am out two or three other evenings a week and that another evening away will be a burden to my family. I have no concern, because I do not have a family. I can do what I want. If you are single and you live at home, your freedom may be restricted because of the time you need to spend with your family. But for the most part, we are free. If you have a desire to begin a certain kind of ministry, you have the freedom to rearrange your schedule to fit that in.

Married people do not have that freedom. There are certain priorities that they have to work around. Singles have more flexibility and freedom.

Single people also have opportunities to further God's kingdom by financial means. They do not have the financial pressures of those who are married and have families. They do not have to think about one or two or three other mouths to feed—just their own. Married people must think in terms of their family when they consider their finances.[2] When we singles get our paychecks, the opportunities for using money are limitless. Imagine the freedom we have to invest our money in God's work. We are missing out on the bliss of being single in this area.

A certain single man has a very special ministry. He has a friend who is a traveling speaker, and this single person calls his friend every week, no matter where his friend is in the country. He does that to encourage his friend over the phone. And they talk and they talk and they talk. Then they pray, and this person's bill is enormous. How can he do it? He does not have anyone else to look out for—just himself—and this is a way that he can use his money to be of encouragement and comfort to other people. What a ministry![3]

A young woman in one of our college Bible studies wanted to go on a missions project a few years ago. Her Bible study group raised $1,000 to send her. Last spring a young man at another Bible study had the opportunity to go on a summer project in Europe, and in a few weeks the Bible study group raised $1,200 to send him. Financially speaking, we can literally "buy up" the opportunities. To us the choice is obvious between spending $18 a month to support an orphan or $18 a month to buy Junior clothing. We can use our money in tremendous ways.

All of us have a certain amount of time on this earth, and we are to utilize this time to the glory of God. If we have the gift of singleness, then it is to our advantage to remain single, because that is the way we will best be able to use our time.

Does that mean that single people do greater works for the Lord than married people? No, Scripture never says that. One's potential as an individual as far as his walk and ministry is concerned lies in being in the will of God. That is the most important consideration. If God has called you to the single life, then that is where your potential lies. If God has called you to marriage, and the majority will marry, that is where your potential lies. It is an individual matter.

Paul is saying this so we might be "free from concern" (verse 32). He wants us to be without care. He does not want us to give our attention to the things of this life in such a way that our time might be used up and the opportunities allowed to slip by. It is as if he is saying, "Let us all have the perspective that the opportunities are restricted and that life and the world are passing away. It is my desire that if you are able to remain single, do so, because I know what it is like to seize the opportunities. I know what it is like to grasp after those opportunities to further God's kingdom. Because I am single, I would recommend it."

If you are able to remain single—excellent. If not, verse 28 again comes into focus. "But if you should marry, you have not sinned." Paul always leaves that out, and he has to because marriage is indeed good. He recommends celibacy, but he allows individuals to choose what they think is suitable for them (the ultimate decision is God's, of course).

If you are able to remain single, stay that way. It is to your advantage.

4

Freedom in Devotion

First Corinthians 7: 32-35 states:

> But I want you to be free from concern. One who is unmarried is concerned about the things of the Lord, how he may please the Lord; but one who is married is concerned about the things of the world, how he may please his wife, and his interests are divided. And the woman who is unmarried, and the virgin, is concerned about the things of the Lord, that she may be holy both in body and spirit; but one who is married is concerned about the things of the world, how she may please her husband. And this I say for your own benefit; not to put a restraint upon you, but to promote what is seemly, and to secure undistracted devotion to the Lord.

Some of you might think that this is similar to verses 29-31. There is a slightly different emphasis. In verses 29-31 Paul recommends the single state in relationship to the opportunities that one has and the utilization of one's time. The single person can take advantage of the opportunities. In verses 32-35 Paul recommends the single state in relation to one's devotion to Jesus Christ. In other words, he is talking about the preoccupation of one's mind—that is, devotion to the Lord. In single living there is a single-mindedness, with no division of interests.

In verses 32-35 we see the reality of single life and the reality of married life. First of all, Paul writes that one who is unmarried is concerned about the things of the Lord, how he may please the Lord. The unmarried person can give his full attention to the things of Jesus Christ. He can give his main thoughts to furthering God's kingdom. His thoughts, desires, dreams, and plans center on the things of the Lord.

He thinks about starting that discipling group, he thinks about beginning that new ministry or that new outreach. He thinks about spending quality time in communion with God. He can center on a meaningful prayer life. His thoughts are on that study of the book in the Bible he has always wanted to study. He thinks about serving his sisters in the family of God. He can ask the Lord what He wants him to do. When the Lord answers, the unmarried person can immediately respond and obey. That is the potential.

It certainly does not mean that every single person is totally devoted to Jesus Christ. But there is that potential for total devotion or undivided loyalty to Jesus Christ. There is single-heartedness. One can concentrate completely on how to please God. He can focus all of his energy, all of his ability, and all of his thoughts totally on God. He is able to commune with Him and serve Him. He is able to secure undistracted devotion to the Lord (verse 35).

Verse 33, however, states: "But one who is married is concerned about the things of the world, how he may please his wife." The reality of married life is that married people are preoccupied with each other. There are certain things that encumber one's mind when married. A married man must concentrate on things concerning his wife. He has to think about how to please his wife. He has to think about meeting her needs. Then the children come, and there must be time given to them.

He has to think about life insurance. He has to think about a bigger house. He has to think about saving money for the children's education. He has to think about meeting the psychological, emotional, and spiritual needs of the family. He is obliged to do all this before the Lord. 1 Timothy 5:8 says: "But if anyone does not provide for his own, and especially for those of his household, he has denied the faith, and is worse than an unbeliever."

Is Paul saying that because a man has to think about all this, that having a wife is bad? No, not at all. Being concerned with the Lord and a wife are not bad. They are both good. But to Paul, the issue at this point is that there are two of them. As Paul says in verse 34: "And his interests are divided." There is an inability for single-mindedness in marriage. The married person is a divided person, having a divided set of cares. The married man must be more occupied with earthly things than one who is single. The single person can secure undistracted devotion to the Lord. He does not have that added responsibility or accountability before the Lord of a family to provide for and protect. Christ alone can be his focus and the sole preoccupation of his mind.

During my early college years I would come home from school and study the Bible. I wanted to learn more about God, so I would read Christian books and spend time meditating on the Lord. I bombarded myself with truth. The same thing was true in my years on staff with a Christian organization. I would come home and would read Christian books. I would then read Scripture and meditate on the person of God. What a freedom in devotion singles have!

These past two years I have experienced this freedom of devotion in a very special way, by doing something that would be hard to do if I were married. I like to go away for two or three days and take my Bible and Stephen Charnock's book on the attributes of God, and I spend the whole time reading and meditating. What a great time! One time I went up to the mountains, and I stayed in a trailer owned by some friends and read 100 pages on the sovereignty of God from Charnock's book. Another time I read on the goodness of God. Recently I had the opportunity to spend a few days in a condominium, where I read Charnock's chapter on the immutability of God. This is freedom in devotion, with my thoughts being totally on Jesus Christ. I would come back from those times of being away, talk to a married brother, and tell him what I did, and he would say, "You know, Allen, I wish I could do that. But it is so hard when you are married." That is what Paul is saying.

Please do not think that Paul is saying that the single state is a more spiritual state simply because a person is undivided in allegiance. Learning how to please your husband or please your wife is a very holy matter. It is very precious in God's eyes and very important. God is delighted when a married individual takes the time and energy to please his wife or her husband. Paul is simply commenting on the reality of a married life and the reality of a single life, not that one is better than the other or more spiritual than the other. He is just saying that there is freedom in devotion in single living.

Verse 34 says: "And the woman who is unmarried, and the

virgin, is concerned about the things of the Lord, that she may be holy both in body and spirit.'' The same thing is true with the unmarried woman as with the unmarried man. The unmarried woman can be like Mary, sitting at Christ's feet, communing with Him and having single-mindedness of devotion. It says that she may be holy or separated. Again, he is not saying that single people are more holy than married people. He is saying that the one who is not married can be separated unto God physically and spiritually. There is no need to satisfy the physical. There are no spiritual encumbrances. It is obvious that this person has the ''gift,'' which we will be examining later. In the single state there is the potential of consecration in body and spirit.

Verse 34 says that a wife's thoughts must center on how to be an encouragement to her husband. She must think about how to be a support to him. She must think about how to be a helper to him. She must think about how to care for her family. But in addition to her responsibility to her husband and her family is the responsibility to be devoted to the Lord. She has to be communing with God; therefore, she has divided concentration.

I was talking to a married woman who said that there is no question that a married person has divided interests. She said, ''I have a baby to think about, and I have a husband to think about. It is consuming.'' Every single woman needs to ask, ''Is marriage what I really want at this time? Am I willing to let my thoughts be given to how to help him, how to support a man? Am I willing to have my thoughts consumed with the cares of a family?'' Some of you are saying, ''Yes! Yes! Yes!'' That is good. That is a good desire.

But others might be saying, ''I have never thought about that before. I guess to be honest with myself at this point in my life, my desires are to have undistracted devotion to the Lord and not have my interests divided. Marriage would not be right for me.'' If you feel that way, that is good. Do not be down on yourself. Marriage may not be for you, or marriage is not for you at this time. Or else, the young man for whom you could joyously sacrifice has not come along yet. Give of yourself to the Lord's person and work. Let your thoughts be lifted up heavenward. Learn to commune with Him and be devoted to Him. Spend your time as an overflow of your communing with Him by serving Him as you never have before.

May each Christian male reader marry a sister who has given herself totally to the Lord's person and work. I trust that you will marry someone whose motivation for holy living has been the Lord, and not a man; whose desire for godliness in the body and the spirit is because she loves the Lord Jesus Christ, and not a man; whose desire has been to please the Lord. Why? In a marriage relationship a man will not always motivate his wife to holiness. Therefore, he does not want her basic motivation for holy living in body and spirit to be himself. It needs to be the Lord.

Something very beautiful can happen in the life of a single person who is not dating on a regular basis and who is single and unattached. God has the freedom to begin developing within him motives for holiness and godliness that are based in Him alone.

One thing we forget as single people is that we are cultivating our married life right now as single people. It will be richer and fuller because of what we are now becoming, or else the opposite will be true. We will gain the dividends in marriage of what we invest now as single people. What we sow now as unmarrieds will be reaped in marriage.

The priority right now is to be in love with Jesus Christ. That should always be the priority but especially now as a single person. What a waste, if the time you begin committing yourself to holiness in body and spirit is the day you say, ''I do.''

Verse 35 says: ''And this I say for your own benefit.'' Paul says that his motive is your good. He says that he does not want to put a restraint upon you. *Restraint* is literally a noose, or slipknot, for hanging or strangling. In urging the Corinthians to remain single, Paul has no intention of restraining a person's liberty. He is not saying that all must take a vow of celibacy. He is only saying what, in his judgment, would be most to their advantage under existing circumstances. His intention is that they secure undistracted devotion to the Lord. Paul wants us to avoid that which would be even the slightest hindrance to our being undistractedly devoted to the Lord.

5

Freedom Through Fulfillment

Having examined 1 Corinthians 7:25-36 we now know why in 7:1 Paul says it is good for a man not to touch a woman. We now know why he says in verse 7 that he wishes that all men were even as he is. We now know why he says in verse 8 to the unmarried and to the widows that it is good for them if they remain even as he is. His reasons are because there is freedom from pressure, freedom to serve, and freedom in devotion when one is single.

In Matthew 19 Jesus lays down strong guidelines for marriage. After doing so, His disciples tell Him in Matthew 19:10 that "if the relationship of the man with his wife is like this, it is better not to marry." In other words, with all that going on, it would be better not to get married to begin with. Jesus says that that is true, but not all men can receive this saying, except to those to whom it has been given. It is good to be single, but not every one can handle that, except those who have been given it. I personally believe that those people who are able to accept it are very, very few.

Does that mean that every Christian who is single and who remains single the rest of his life has been given this special something by God? I do not think so. Many people remain single for reasons other than the fact that they were given this gift by the Lord.

Some remain single because of the fears that accompany marriage. There are some who remain single because of an unhappy childhood. Maybe they were ill-treated by others in the family. These things have conditioned many persons against the prospect of marriage, but that certainly cannot be what Jesus is talking about. Some remain single because of their dislike for or distrust of the opposite sex. But that is not what Jesus is talking about.

Some people choose the single life for other reasons. One extreme case is found in Chrysostom's letter to a young man who planned to marry a beautiful girl. Chrysostom told the man to consider what lay behind the lovely face and figure. This is what he wrote in his letter.

> The groundwork of this corporeal beauty is nothing else but phlegm and blood and humor and bile, and the fluid of masticated food . . . If you consider what is stored up inside those beautiful eyes, and that straight nose, and the mouth and cheeks, you will affirm the well-shaped body to be nothing else than a whited sepulchre . . . Moreover, when you see a rag with any of these things on it, such as phlegm, or spittle, you cannot bear to touch it even with the tips of your fingers, nay you cannot endure looking at it; are you then in a flutter of excitement about the storehouses and repositories of these things?[1]

Believe it or not, that letter persuaded that young man that a life of celibacy might be best after all. But that is not what Jesus is talking about. What is He talking about? What is that thing that is "given" to enable someone to be single? What are indications of having what is "given?"

We have to look again at 1 Corinthians 7, because Paul is going to be an interpreter of Christ's words at this point. Paul is going to help us understand what this gift is.

Paul has great balance. He realizes there are some who have it, and yet he realizes that there are some, or should I say many, who do not. He realizes that this ability of living without marriage is not given to everyone. To some people it is not a gift. It is absolute torture. He realizes that for some people it is not as easy being single as it is for him. He says, "Yet I wish that all men were even as I myself am [verse 7]. However, each man has his own gift from God. One in this manner, and another in that."

Now the word "gift" is *charisma,* and it means an endowment of grace, an enablement, or a special gift of God. Paul says that each person has a special endowment of grace that makes his mind and body suited to the condition that God has called him. Each one has his own gift. Consequently, opposite courses for different individuals are right. One man can be like Paul, another man different from Paul. Paul is not about to say that being different from him is wrong, because what you might have is as much from God as what he has. No doubt Paul is speaking about the giftedness in the area of singleness and marriage.

Paul has something specific in mind when he talks about remaining single or getting married. He says in verse 8, "But I say to the unmarried and to widows that it is good for them if they remain even as I. But if they do not have self-control . . ." The Greek word for self-control, *egkratevontai,* is based on the stem word *krat*, which denotes power or lordship. Being in the middle voice, it refers to power over one's self, to hold oneself in and to control oneself, to possess in oneself the power of controlling oneself.

The idea is to have power or dominion over all things and over oneself, to be inwardly strong. The word was used in the Septuagint, the Greek translation of the Old Testament, to denote that one had gained control of something. In Genesis 43:31 it is used in the sense of an individual's composing himself or having control over himself. It is used in classical Greek as having reference to superiority to every desire.

The word is not found at all in the gospels, but is used in 1 Corinthians 9:25, "And everyone who competes in the games exercises self-control in all things." Paul compares himself with an athlete at this point and says, "That for the sake of the goal for which he strives, the commission which he has been given, the task which he must fulfill, he restrains or he refrains from all the things which might offend or hamper."[2] He abstains from sensual indulgences, because he has a goal for which he is aiming. When used in the negative in 7:9, "If they do not have self-control," he means lack of power over oneself or absence of self-control. What is meant by this failure to have power over oneself is partly explained by the next phrase. If a person does not have self-control, Paul exhorts, "Let them marry, for it is better to marry than to burn."

What does "burn" mean? First of all, it is in the present tense so it implies a recurring condition of burning on, or continuing to burn. It is in the middle voice, so it has the idea of burning in oneself. The word is *pyrousthai,* which is related to the word *pyre,* or fire, and it means to burn or be inflamed. The *New International Dictionary of New Testament Theology* says that it is to be inflamed, and it is used of the heat of emotions. That same word, interesting enough, is used in 2 Corinthians 11:29 where Paul says, "Who is led into sin without my intense concern?" Or literally, Who is led into sin without my burning? Paul says he has an inflaming, an intensity about him when someone sins. But in 7:9 it is used figuratively of sexual desire.

In the *Theological Dictionary of the New Testament* Gerhard Kittel and Gerhard Friedrich say that it means "to be consumed with the fire of sexual desire." It means to burn in oneself with the fire of sexual desire. It implies a prolonged and painful struggle. The *American Commentary on the New Testament* says, "To be inflamed with unsatisfied passion." In his *Word Studies in the New Testament* M. Vincent says, "Continuance in unsatisfied desire." It is the excitement of unsatisfied desires that causes some to be disturbed or to feel weak.

Paul says that for these people it is better to marry than to burn. Paul says to the Corinthians that if they do not possess power over themselves, if there is a constant inflaming of sexual desire, let them marry. A single, definite act of marriage is better than the recurring condition of burning.

The next question is: Why is it better? Paul states in verse 1 of chapter 7 that singleness is good. But he immediately asserts that there is the danger that the single person may be tempted to satisfy bodily desires by illicit sexual practices. He says in verse 2 that it is good to be single, not to have sexual relationships, but, because of immoralities, let each man have his own wife and let each woman have her own husband. In other words, Paul is saying to get married.

"Immoralities" is in the plural and points to the manifold sexual vices in Corinth. It refers to immoralities that would result if marriage were prohibited. In Paul's day, the immoral life-style of the Corinthian culture made it hard for unmarried people to be pure. The loose attitude in Corinth made immorality and fornication a persistent temptation. Corinth was the vice capital of the world and, being a seaport, was a meeting place of all nationalities offering all the vices. In fact, in the temple of Aphrodite there were 1,000 prostitute priestesses who "ministered" in this pagan temple.

To live as a Corinthian meant to live in luxury and immorality. In fact, the verb *corinthianized* meant to have sex with a prostitute. So these Christians were facing unique sexual temptations, and they were writing Paul for advice. Corinth was like downtown Hollywood and Las Vegas combined. We have some idea of what it was like just by looking in the newspaper or driving in Hollywood, but it was probably worse than we could even imagine. To Paul, marriage is not a concession to fleshly appetite. He is not regarding marriage as an escape mechanism for those too weak to bridle their passions. He is only pointing out that a potential result of marriage is that one could avoid persistent temptation in the area of sex. Therefore, celibacy is not recommended to any except those who have that gift of *egkrateia,* or self-control. To many people it would prove to be a snare to remain single. For many people it is not good to *not* touch a woman. It does not matter how bad the present distress is, it may be better to get married.

Why is it better to marry? Because marriage once and for all is better than continuous consuming desire. The state of marriage is morally allowable and sinless, and the marriage bed is undefiled. But the state of constant burning is a potential trouble to one's life, and inasmuch as the demands and temptations of man's physical nature are what they are, he advises the average man or woman to marry. It is good not to marry, but better on account of immoralities to marry than to have inflamed and unsatisfied desires. Do not think that Paul is encouraging Christians to marry for purposes of sex alone. That is absurd, but it is one factor to consider. It is better to marry than to continually struggle with the fire of sexual desire.

The phrase in verse 9 "let them marry," according to Dana and Mantey's *Manual on Greek Grammar,* is an imperative of permission. It implies consent. Paul is saying, "You're asking me what to do with unmarried people who are in this condition. Here is my answer. I give my permission that those people marry. It is OK if they marry; they have not sinned."

It is hard to know the exact situation that brought about this issue of the unmarried and why Paul had to answer that he gave his consent. Possibly this is in response to the talk within the Corinthian church that you were more spiritual if you did not marry or if you did not have sexual relationships. There was a group of people who thought that was right, and maybe Paul was saying, "Listen. Do not let anyone impose something on you like a vow of celibacy if you are not gifted that way. Do not let anyone do that. If you do not have absolute control over your emotions so that you are not bothered or distracted, then it is no time to think about remaining single for the rest of your life. If you do not have the ability, do not make rash vows, and do not let anyone talk you into remaining single; it is better to marry than to aggravate those suppressed drives by mandatory abstinence." There was even some talk that, in a marriage relationship, sexual fulfillment was wrong. That is why Paul says in verse 5 to stop depriving one another of sexual fulfillment. Do not think it is more spiritual to abstain from sexual relations unless certain conditions are met—

that is, unless you both agree it is for a stated time and the purpose is for prayer (verse 5). But otherwise, come back together. Why? "Lest Satan tempt you because of your lack of self-control" (verse 5). So that element was present in the Corinthian church.

Very much tied into this is Paul's statement in verse 36. Paul applies this principle of lack of self-control in marriage to one group of those mentioned in the unmarried category—young single women. Back then, marriages were arranged by the fathers in both the Jewish and Roman cultures. For example, Abraham selected a wife for Isaac, and that process continued until around the year 500 B.C., when the custom of marriage brokers developed. When you had a daughter that had come to the age where you wanted her married, you went to the marriage broker and said, "This is what I want for my girl." The marriage broker would say something like, "Have I got someone for you in Joppa!" It may not have been *exactly* like that, but that was the idea.

It is also apparent that even though the marriage was arranged by the family, usually there was some kind of love relationship that existed between the two people. It was not a complete surprise on the wedding day.

In 1 Corinthians they still have that pattern for a father-arranged marriage. Therefore, Paul says in verse 36, "If any man thinks"—that is, if any father—"thinks that he is acting unbecomingly toward his virgin daughter . . ." A father says, "You know, the world is distressing, and there are reasons for remaining single, and I like what Paul says. It is good to be single. I think I will consecrate my daughter to the Lord and devote her life to the building of the kingdom of God. I am going to devote her to that so she can be holy in body and spirit."

Now the father thinks that he is doing her a favor, but he realizes at some point that he is acting unfairly. Why? Verse 36 again. "If any man thinks that he is acting unbecomingly toward his virgin daughter, if she should be of full age . . ." Literally, "full age" means "overripe." In other words, if she reaches sexual maturity when she has all the sexual sensitivity. "And if it must be so, let him do what he wishes, he does not sin; let her marry." Literally, let *them* marry. Sound familiar? Same expression as verse 9. The implication here is a strong sexual urge.

You may be single and may be saying, "These advantages of being single are great. I can do this and do that, more time, no pressure." Do not make yourself out to be a hero and forget marriage, especially if you are not fit for single living— especially if by remaining single you expose yourself to constant temptation. Paul says to the fathers, "Do not impose something on your daughters that they will not be able to handle." The last thing that Paul wants to do is to encourage someone into a position against which his nature would unceasingly rebel, and thereby make life one chronic temptation. He is saying that it is permissible for people who lack the power of self-control in matters of sex to marry and thus solve the problem related to sex impulses.[3]

The *Jewish Encyclopedia* said this: "Judaism . . . regards celibacy as an unnatural state conducive to constant sinful thought, and it advises rather that a man marry at about the age of 20, so that he will have the peace and purity of mind to serve God and study the Torah, without being distracted by heroic efforts to submerge natural impulses."[3] It is better to get married so that we will not be distracted by heroic efforts to submerge our natural impulses. If one is going around flaming with desire on the inside, then Paul says marriage is permitted. There is no point in saying, "I am remaining single for the cause of Christ." No, he says, "Consider marriage. It will bring about the fulfillment of physical desire."

So what is the gift? What is this *charisma* of *egkrateia*? Divine enablement given to control and not to be consumed with sexual desires outside of marriage. It is an ability not to be preoccupied with sex in the sense that it becomes a distraction to your daily life. When you are not literally overwrought with the inability to fulfill that physical desire, you probably have that gift. If your sexual desires and drives are manageable, you probably have that gift. If you have this gift, Paul's statement in verse 2 would be meaningless to you—"because of immoralities."

Fornications and immoralities would probably not be a problem to you. You are a person with self-control. You are not consumed by desire. You can experience complete freedom in serving God undistractedly. It is also important to note that to "have self-control" is in the present tense. If the pattern of your life is such that you do not possess power over your sexual desires, and what characterizes your life is distraction because of unfulfilled sexual desires, then for you the following statement is true—you are better off being married than being in a state where your desires are inflamed.

The *Expositors Bible* says, "If any man's temperament be such that he cannot settle undistractedly to his work without marrying; if he is restless and ill at ease, and full of natural cravings which make him think much of marriage, and make him feel sure he would be less distracted in married life—then, says Paul, let such an one by all means marry . . . I permit every man to marry who believes he will be the better of marrying."[4]

But if your life is such that you *do* possess power over yourself physically, that you are not distracted, that you are not restless, that you are not ill at ease, it is my recommendation that you remain single. Why? Because of the advantages— freedom from pressure, freedom to serve, and freedom in devotion.

One can readily see how this gift of self-mastery regarding one's sexual desires was valuable to Paul. He could travel all over the place as an apostle and be content doing that. He had complete sexual self-mastery and could remain without a wife and a family.

People know they have this gift because they are content. Desires for marriage and sexual desires are not ongoing distractions. Regarding sexual desires, they are not brought to a frustration point. Thoughts of marriage are not the consuming thought patterns of the life. A person I spoke with said he believed he has the gift, but to him it does not mean that you are unaware of what is going on. When an attractive young lady walks by, he takes notice. It also does not mean that at times he does not think, *It would be nice to be married*. Even then marriage is not seen as a fulfillment of sexual desires but rather as a cure to loneliness.

But as he said, these thoughts do not become consuming thoughts. If they ever did become consuming, then it would be time to think about marriage. You ask, Is there ever a struggle? He said, "In no true life situation do you have everything going for you; that is sheer folly. There is no utopia for anybody, but there is a tolerance where you can handle it comfortably. And if that is so, you have the gift. There is a certain percentage of feeling that you are missing out, but the good outweighs that. If you cannot handle that comfortably, then it is a good indication you do not have the gift."

In other words, if you become unglued and the end result is that you cannot handle singleness, you are probably a prime candidate for marriage. You say, "I cannot conceive of not being bothered. I cannot conceive of my sexual desires never being an ongoing distraction." That is a good indication that you do not have the *charisma* of *egkrateia,* the gift of self-control. If you do not have that power of control and you do feel enticed, then you are probably not a good candidate for a life of single living. It is better for you to marry than live in a state of inflamed sexual desires, always being tempted.

But you say, "Everyone must feel frustrated." No, everyone does not. Not those whom God has gifted. Mark Lee writes:

> The assumption on the part of active sex-oriented persons that all other men and women are compelled by the same drives is unproved. Society at large, however, presumes that sex drives are universal and the norm for human beings. If an individual seems to manage well without sex or marriage, that person is viewed with much skepticism. The general population finds it hard to believe that any significant segment will not seek sexual fulfillment.[5]

There is a segment that will not seek sexual fulfillment—those whom God has gifted. You might be reading this and saying to yourself, "I am not frustrated sexually. I am very content." If you are, do not think you are strange. Perhaps you are one that God has specially and uniquely gifted for singleness. If that is the case, then seek His face regarding your mission in life and give yourself to it.

By now you are seeing why it is so important that single people not be pushed into marriage. Some people want to play

Cupid all the time, applying the pressure. "You must get married! You cannot go through life being single." Single people should not be pushed, because God has given some single people the gift of *egkrateia,* and if so, then maybe being married is in violation of God's very best for their lives. Even though God looks very favorably on marriage, and it is for the majority, it is not for everyone. Why? Because God has given some people the gift of being single. They do not need to be married to fulfill God's will. In fact, some need to stay single if they are to fulfill God's will to the very fullest.

I want to give you some statements as to what Paul is *not* saying here that might help clarify a few points. First, Paul is not equating the lack of self-control with a life-style of lustful thinking and fornication. There is never a justification for immorality on the basis that you feel that you do not have the gift. "God did not gift me. I am burning; therefore I must fornicate." To burn does not mean that you are flaring out in lustful acts, but rather that you are consumed with inward desire. The idea is that you sense you are in a battle, but not that you are losing it. Burning is unfulfilled desire, not lustful acts.

Paul has something to say about people who find themselves fornicating, and it is not to get married. Paul's words to that person are very clear. First Corinthians 5:11 says not to associate with any so-called brother if he should be an immoral person. First Corinthians 6:9 states, "Do not be deceived; neither fornicators, nor idolaters . . . shall inherit the kingdom of God." First Corinthians 6:18 says that we are to flee immorality. That person is not even at a point to consider marriage. That person needs to clean up his life.

Paul did not say, "You are fornicating, so I think it would be a good idea for the two of you to marry.'' He said to flee immorality, abstain from sexual immorality, and behave properly. Day by day through God's power and Word one gains victory over illicit lust. Paul is not saying, ''Because you are always led into sin, get married.'' No! ''If you are sinning, stop sinning. If you are fornicating, stop fornicating.'' Our priority as single people is to move toward the mastery of our sexual desires. God wants us to move toward obedience in this area. By a series of proper choices we can move in the direction of victory.

Maybe you are saying, ''Wait a second. How can I know whether I have this gift of self-control?'' Let us suppose you have two people desirous of being obedient in this area of sexual purity. The one with the gift will come to a point where he or she feels very comfortable physically. The one without the gift can be doing the same thing, can be memorizing the same Scripture as the other person, can be as accountable to someone else as the other young man or woman, and yet to him or her there still is an uncomfortable feeling. There still is a distraction. Why? Because one has the gift, the other does not.

You see the same thing with any two people with different gifts. For example, you have two people learning how to teach the Word of God. Both are taught the same principles of communication, both go through the same courses, but as they begin to apply what they have learned, one truly feels at peace in the role of a teacher. He feels very comfortable teaching because God has called him to it. There is a peace. The other person is totally frustrated. He feels very uncomfortable in front of a group, cannot communicate effectively, and feels out of place. Why? That person does not have the gift of teaching.

The analogy breaks down because not everyone is asked by God to pursue the gift of teaching, but everyone is asked by God to pursue holiness and sanctification. As we all pursue holiness in the area of mastery over our sexual desires, some will be content, with the struggle growing less and less. Why? They have the gift. For others, try as they might through God's power, it is hard. It is a battle. It is not so much that they are disobedient to God as that they do not have the gift. If that is the case and there is not a sin issue in your life, you can assume that you are one that needs to be married. But in no way does that release you from the responsibility you have to purify yourself right now as a single person. In the future, either the struggle will be gone, you will feel comfortable, and have peace and contentment, or else marriage will probably come into the picture. In the meantime, a person's priority should be to walk with God and be obedient to Him.

Second, he is not saying that if you are able to control sexual desires and live comfortably with yourself, then you can never marry. Maybe you are saying, "My desires are not strong. They are not a distraction. I do feel comfortable. Maybe I will never marry." That is not necessarily true. There is more to being married than fulfillment of sexual desires. Marriage is for companionship, for mutual growth, and many other reasons. Paul would say that he prefers that you remain single, but you have not sinned if you marry.

If you have the gift, consider remaining single because there is freedom from pressure, freedom to serve, and freedom in devotion. But you are able to get married if you want to. In fact, this gift of self-control is valuable in the marriage state because it frees someone from much temptation, as verse 5 suggests.

In looking at this from another angle, there is no reason why those whom Jesus said in Matthew 19 were born physically incapable of sexual intercourse (and whose sex organs will never become functional) could not marry. This is, of course, unless, as Mark Lee puts it, "Frustration relative to physical intimacy would become excessively strong."[6]

Related to this is the question, Is the gift of self-control permanent? The Bible does not say. The gift for the married status may be changed in a person. It appears that Isaac led an unblemished, celibate life for a time until he was thirty, but afterward he was called into marriage. There are some singles who live content physically and socially, but then after a while they marry. Who knows what exactly takes place in a person's life? Maybe in God's will, when His plan for that person as a single person is over, the desires intensify physically and socially, and his giftedness changes. For example, there is no problem physically, but at some point the desires intensify, and the Lord brings the right young man or woman along. Or else maybe there is no problem physically at all. Then the Lord brings the right young man or lady, and then the desires intensify. But it appears that the gift may be changed in a person.

Third, he is not saying anything as to the time that an individual should get married. He is not saying to marry the next person you date. His intention is not to push people into marriage. He is not putting a time limit on it. He is simply establishing the principle that if physical desires are there and are tempting, and you are not able to experience mastery over them as a pattern of life, it is a good indication that you should get married. When you should get married and to whom is another question.

Fourth, Paul is not saying that the primary reason for marriage is to avoid fornication. Remember, Paul is answering specific questions. He was asked the question, ''Should everyone be single?'' He is saying that everyone cannot be single because of the problems of unfulfilled sexual desires. What is in question here is not so much the *reasons* marriage was instituted but rather the *persons* for whom it is necessary. The issue here is not the reason God instituted marriage, but rather that, if you are this kind of person, marriage is probably for you. If fulfillment of sexual desire is the only reason you want to marry, you will be in more trouble once married than you are now as a single person. There is more to marriage than the physical. The reason to be married is not based on the physical. It is based on God's will, which is determined by a number of factors—mutual love, parental approval, nonviolation of biblical standards of remarriage, and other reasons as well. Unfulfilled, physical desires need to be a part of total desire to have a wife or a husband.

Another point is that this gift goes hand in hand with ministry and service for the kingdom. This is the spiritual factor. Jesus pointed out that some men have a tendency not to marry because they are motivated in a certain direction. When spiritual zeal is added to such a tendency, then there is apparently little struggle in the natural desire to marry. I am not sure which comes first, the self-control or involvement in a ministry.

Jesus does say in Matthew 19:12 that there are eunuchs who made themselves eunuchs for the sake of the kingdom of God. A person's choice to remain single is related to effective service for God. Some people have dedicated themselves to single status in order to perform certain spiritual activities for the Lord. Single status makes possible having a more concentrated ministry for the Lord, and there are some people who could not do what they are doing now if they were married. They desire the single state in order to fulfill that to which God has called them so that the kingdom of God may be furthered. To this person it is more important to do what he or she is doing than being married. Marriage would be too much of a distraction. They are single and are totally given over to what God has called them to do. They are fulfilled. There is a great measure of control over sexual desire; anticipated devotion to the Lord is so fulfilling that one's physical desires are not even an issue. God compensates for them by granting fulfillment in another area. Maybe that sense of fulfillment in a person's life completely outweighs the need for having another human being of the opposite sex fulfill him.

One problem single people face is that they do not know what it is to have that sense of fulfillment that comes from devotion to the Lord because they have never completely given themselves over to an undistracted kind of life-style. God may have unspeakable joy waiting for you if you give yourself completely to Him.

There are two responses to what has been written. One person is saying, "There is freedom in the single life and I love it." There is no tension regarding the single life as you are completely fulfilled as a person. You are challenged and motivated. If that is you, continue that way. Do not let anyone talk you out of it.

But there is another response: "I hear what you are saying, but there is a tension within me. I do not have this gift. Marriage looks very good to me. I desire to be married, but I am not. You say that single people can be undistractedly devoted to the Lord? Well, I'm single, but I have many distractions, like, Who is she? Where is she? If that is you, you fall into the group of individuals I am addressing in the next section. You are a prime candidate for one experiencing the blisters of the single life.

PART II

The Blisters
of the Single Life

Introduction

Why is it so difficult to deal with one's desires for marriage? One answer lies in the fact that marriage is a very good thing. It is good to be single, but it is also good to be married. Jerome inaccurately interpreted 1 Corinthians 7:1 by saying that since it is good to be single, it is wrong to be married. That is not right at all! It is a very good thing to be married. It is not wrong to have a desire to be married. God intended marriage to be the norm.

Genesis 2:18 says, "It is not good for the man to be alone; I will make him a helper suitable for him." Proverbs 18:22 says, "He who finds a wife finds a good thing." Hebrews 13:4 says, "Let marriage be held in honor among all." 1 Timothy 4:3 says that prohibition of marriage is one of the signs of the great apostasies. First Corinthians 7:2 says that marriage is acceptable. In Ephesians 5:22 and following, Paul elevates marriage to the loftiest position by employing it as a type of union between Christ and His believers.

God looks favorably on marriage, and there are many who will find it easier to serve God in the married state. Those persons would be more distracted single than married. Many have found their usefulness to God increased and enhanced by marriage. In marriage one's needs to love and be loved are met. There is an intimate companionship in marriage. That is a great support and a source of stength.

One writer says, "God intended man and woman to be mutually enriching to one another. He planned that husband and wife should experience a thorough sharing of all of life together, that they should support one another and encourage one another and talk together and walk together and laugh and love and weep and worship—together. Together they were made to reflect God's image. They were made for each other and for Him."[1] "There is a shared intimacy experienced together that is possible with no one else."[2] Marriage is a very good thing, and for most, God's plan involves marriage.

However, if we believe that we do not have that gift of self-control, then at some point in our lives we will probably experience some tension regarding our singleness. That tension will exist because the desires are present, yet the fulfillment is absent. The degree of that tension and struggle will be different for each of us. Because of this, it is important to consider the blisters of the single life.

Two points need to be made by way of introduction. First, James 1:5 says, "But if any of you lacks wisdom, let him ask of God, who gives to all men generously and without reproach, and it will be given to him." The context of this verse has to do with the subject of trials, and certainly, for many single people, the single state can be a trial. God says that if we have encountered a trial, we can ask Him for wisdom so that we might have His perspective on that trial and thus know what to do in that trial to gain victory. James says we can ask of God because God is a certain kind of God. He is a giving-to-all-men-generously kind of God. The word *generous* means "to spread out or to reach." The idea is that God's hand is stretched forth, and He wants to give without reserve. In this context, He wants to give wisdom.

God is also a non-reproaching God. In other words, God does not heap insults upon the man who comes to Him in need. He does not tell us that we come to Him too often or ask too much. He is not that way at all. He does not scold us because we cannot understand the nature of the trial. God wants us to come and invites us to come, that we might ask Him for wisdom in difficult situations.

Second, we must not interpret Scripture in light of our experience, but interpret our experience in light of Scripture. If the Scripture says that this is what my experience can be, but on the other hand my experience contradicts that, then something is wrong. With the Scripture? No. With my experience. If God says a certain experience is possible, and I am not experiencing it, then something needs to happen. That is not saying that God expects us to change overnight; for most of us the change is very gradual. Our thinking is renewed, and victory is increasing day by day. God expects me to recognize my lack and trust His power to change me.

6

Looking at God's Attributes

We singles have heard probably every exhortation in the Word of God regarding our singleness. We have been exhorted to wait on the Lord, trust in the Lord, depend on the Lord, commit our ways to the Lord, relax in the Lord, be content, not fret, not sweat, accept God's will for our lives, be joyful, and the list goes on and on. However, these exhortations will not do. We need something beyond these commands. When I am struggling, I need to know and hear something beyond "just trust in the Lord" or "wait on the Lord" or "commit your way to the Lord." We need to know *what* we must do but also *why* we must do it. We need answers that will get right to the core of the issue. Merely an exhortation or a command will not last over the long haul. We need truth that we can go back to, saying, "Because this is true, I *can* trust, I *can* wait, I *can* depend, and I *can* commit my way unto the Lord."

In the past few years the Lord has driven me back to a truth that is without a doubt the greatest or most encouraging truth I have learned—God has driven me back to the truth about Himself. The answer is found in Himself. As single people we need to view our single state through the perspective of His attributes. We need to view our situation through the perspective of His person and nature. This provides the *why* behind all the exhortations and the commands to fret not, wait, trust, depend, and commit.

I approach a problem or struggle this way: If I am finding it hard to trust God in a situation, then my problem is that I do not know Him. To me, it is that simple. Psalm 9:10 says, "Those who know Thy name will put their trust in Thee." Much of the difficulty we have in trusting God is because we do not know Him; if we knew Him, we would trust Him. There is some truth about His person we do not know. Knowing God is without a doubt the key to practical Christian living.

You might argue that knowing who God is does not completely answer the question, *Why* am I single? That is true. I cannot tell you the reason you are single, but I can tell you who God is; in the end that will be sufficient.

When I was young and became sick, I would tell my father. My greatest need at that point was not to hear ten reasons why I was sick, but rather, I wanted to know that my dad loved me, would take me to the doctor, and would pay the bill when it came. I needed to know that he had my best interests in mind and that he had power to do something about it. In the same way, trust in God does not say that we need to know all the reasons that something is exactly the way it is. Trust implies that we will believe that God is who He says He is, and we will trust in His promises and His person.

God can be trusted because of who He is; if we spent more time meditating on the person of God, we would have a better understanding of our lives and would spend less time resenting God or hating God or envying other people's happiness. What attributes can we look to? I would like to focus on two: God's goodness and His wisdom.

The goodness of God is His inclination to deal well and bountifully with His creatures (Psalms 25:8; 106:1; 119:68; 145:9; Mark 10:18). This goodness of God is infinite. It knows no limits. "Divine goodness," Stephen Charnock says, "communicates itself to a vast number of creatures in various degrees; to angels, glorified spirits, men on earth, to every creature, and when it hath communicated all that the present world is capable of, there is still less displayed than left to enrich another world. All possible creatures are not capable of exhausting the wealth, the treasures, that divine bounty is filled with."[1]

God's goodness causes Him to be active in manifesting or communicating that goodness. His goodness is not an idle thing. He does not keep it to Himself, but He communicates or shares it. His goodness tells me that God desires my highest welfare and that God is for me.

This is such an important attribute for us to know; single people can often feel cheated because God has withheld something from them. Have you ever felt that way? True peace lies in knowing that God is good, and His goodness is such that He would never cheat anyone. He deals bountifully with His children.

One verse in particular that is very helpful is Psalm 84:11: "For the Lord God is a sun and shield; the Lord gives grace and glory; no good thing does He withhold from those who walk uprightly. O Lord of Hosts, how blessed is the man who trusts in Thee!" No good thing does He withhold from those who walk uprightly.

Elisabeth Elliot, wife of Jim Elliot, a missionary who was killed by the Auca Indians in Ecuador, was asked in an interview, "What about patience? In your writing, you mentioned waiting for your first husband, Jim, to decide if he wanted to marry you. What sort of guidance did God provide for you during that time?" This is her answer:

> I think one of the most important verses from the Psalms is, "No good thing will He withhold from them that walk uprightly." Now the giving or the withholding of gifts is in God's sovereign care. But my responsibility is in walking uprightly. God knows if marriage is a good thing for me. It certainly looks good to me, but God knows if it is really a good thing— if it will contribute to His purposes for me. Now, can I believe that He will give it to me in His time? I have to trust Him, and I have to walk uprightly. Those are my two responsibilities. I am not to be sitting in impatience and fret and worry, wondering if I am ever going to get married or get anybody. That is none of my business—any more than it is my business of the use God makes of my gifts. I turn them over to Him. My life is His. However, the act of the will of turning one's life over to God is not, by any means, necessarily accompanied by good feelings. From day to day I had to go on by faith, believing that if Jim Elliot was the man God had for me, He would bring him to me. If he wasn't, then maybe God had somebody else and maybe He didn't.[2]

God has our best interests in mind because He is a good God. The goodness of God assures us that if we truly do not have the gift of self-control, then God in His goodness will provide in some way. But His goodness also says that God will withhold something from us if He knows it would not be good for us. His goodness provides for us, but it also protects us.

Maybe the reason God has withheld marriage is because He knows our reasons for wanting it are not pure. Here are some reasons. "I want to be married so I will not be single." "I want to get married so I can have my needs met." "I want to be married so I can solve all my problems." Maybe God has withheld marriage because He has a certain ministry opportunity ahead that will demand full attention and devotion, and marriage would be a distraction.

Do you realize that God is not withholding good from us right now in our single state? If we are trusting and walking uprightly, God is not withholding good from us right now. Maybe the good that God is *not* withholding from us is the rich communion with Jesus Christ that often comes from a life that experiences need because of an unfulfilled desire. Maybe the good that God is not withholding from us now is the genuineness of our prayer life that seeks God from the depths of our beings because of our unfulfilled desires. Do you ever find yourself on your knees crying out to God? God must be pleased with those prayers we offer up to Him.

Maybe the good that God is not withholding is the humility that results when we are confronted with the reality of our unfulfilled desires. Or maybe the good that God is not withholding is the daily clinging to Him that says, "God, I need You. I cannot make it." Or maybe the good that God is not withholding from us now is the richness of fellowship that results when Christians with similar struggles get together and share together and pray together. Or maybe the good that God is not withholding from us now is the sufficiency of His grace.

Paul was given a thorn in the flesh (2 Corinthians 12:7). Literally, the "thorn" means the stake on which offenders were impaled. Therefore, Paul was thinking of a body helplessly impaled and painfully held down. We do not know exactly what that thorn was, but we do know what that thorn was by way of principle. A thorn is anything in your life that reminds you of your weakness.[3]

A thorn may be a disappointment, a physical illness, a tragedy, a discouragement, and to some, a thorn is their single state. There will be those moments in our lives when we will feel absolutely helpless and weak. Our initial response is: "God, I cannot handle it! Remove it! It is keeping me from being all that You want me to be." God says, "No, I have something better for you to experience. I want to open the door to a new dimension of My grace. The best thing I can do is to give you a thorn so that you can experience more and more of My grace. My grace is sufficient for you, for My power is perfected in weakness."

What is "grace"? Grace is divine enablement. It is the aid of the Holy Spirit. It is the sufficiency of God. God says that His strength is brought to completeness in our weakness. The weaker we are, the more conspicuous is His strength in sustaining us. Human weakness provides the opportunity for divine power.

Very soon I become aware that anything that makes me pray is a blessing.[4] How can it be a blessing? When did God ever have your attention more than when you were feeling weak? When were you more desperate? When have you cried out to God more?

Often the presence of need has thrown me more completely on the sufficiency and grace of God. We say, "Marriage." God says, "My grace." We say, "I cannot handle this weakness." God says, "My power is perfected in your weakness." We say, "I want a change of circumstances." God says, "I want a change of perspective." I soon begin to realize how far off I am regarding Paul's desire in Philippians 3. He wanted to know Christ and the power of His resurrection. Often I have to admit that I am more interested in a change of circumstances than I am in experiencing the sufficiency of Christ. At that point God begins to show me where my heart really is. Am I interested in knowing Him? Maturity must certainly be when one is able to say as Paul said, "Most gladly, therefore, I will rather boast about my weaknesses that the power of Christ may dwell in me."

God has my best interests in mind. He is inclined to deal well with us, and although His ways are not our ways, and although I would do things differently than God, still I know that He is good.

The second attribute that has been very encouraging to me is the wisdom of God. God's wisdom is the ability to devise perfect ends and to achieve those ends with the most perfect means (Job 9:4; 12:13; Daniel 2:20; Romans 16:27). It is the power to see and choose the best and highest goal with the surest means of attaining that goal. God always strives for the best possible ends and chooses the best means for the realization of His purposes. J. I. Packer says, "Wisdom is the power to see, and the inclination to choose, the best and highest goal, together with the surest means of attaining it."[5]

What is the best end? There is none more excellent than God; therefore, nothing can be an end except God Himself. He is the end of all. Romans 11:36 says: "For from Him and through Him and to Him are all things. To Him be the glory forever. Amen." It says "from Him"—God is the source of all things; "through Him"—God is the sustainer of all things; and "to Him"—God is the end of all things, with the greatest end being His glory. God is after His glory.

When God is glorified, we are benefited. Your single state is the best place for you to be right now, and God is using your single state as one means to get you to that expected end, His glory. What is so beautiful about all this is that God's ways and actions are determined by a will guided by reason. God's actions are not rash; Ephesians 1:11 says that He is guided by the counsel of His will. The word *counsel* means that one is deliberating on something, looking at all the possibilities, discussing it, and reasoning it through. Of course, God does not have to deliberate in Himself since He already knows that which is best. The word is used for our sake to signify that God does nothing without reason and understanding. It is not a decision where one is arbitrarily chosen to be single and another to be married. God's will for our lives is guided by reason. He has the best end, and He has the best means to get us to that end.

- The very God who does not have to go outside Himself to search out wisdom and who does not need our brains to tell Him to think wisely, any more than He needs our hands and strength to execute His wishes . . .
- The very God who needs no counsel and receives no counsel from any, who is the only fountain of wisdom to others, who is the source of all wisdom, who knows all things clearly, all things possible, all things actual, who knows all possible contingencies, and has foresight of all possible events and situations that may occur . . .
- The very God who never fails at anything He designs and who is infinitely wise in all things . . .
- The very God whose wisdom is without increase or decrease, whose decisions are drawn out of the infinite trea-

sury of wisdom in Himself, whose actions are done with a reason behind them . . .

- The very God who is incomprehensibly wise, who performs all things sovereignly by His will, yet does all things wisely by His understanding . . .
- The very God who willed the entrance of sin, not because of sin itself, but because He knew His wisdom could order it to some greater good . . .
- The very God who by an infinite act of wisdom takes sin, works it out to an end of which man never dreamed, which the devil could never imagine, and which sin in its own nature could never attain . . .
- The very God who by an infinite wisdom used Satan to bring about His own purposes by allowing Satan to tempt Christ that He might sympathize with our weakness; who let Satan inspire men to crucify Christ only for that very act to be used to make Christ a Redeemer of men . . .
- The very God who in infinite wisdom takes the crime of the cross and turns it into the possibility of eternal life . . .
- The very wise God who in His infinite wisdom has taken the messes we have made of our lives and is now making masterpieces out of them . . .
- The very God of whom Paul writes: "Oh, the depth of the riches both of the wisdom and knowledge of God! How unsearchable are His judgments and unfathomable His ways . . ."
- The very God who time and time again has proved Himself to be a God who knows what He is doing . . . This very God who alone is infinitely wise has said, "You are to be single right now!"

We may not know the exact reason we are single, because

many of God's reasons are locked up in Himself, and often He chooses not to let us know. But we certainly know that His reasons are not arbitrary. When it gets right down to it, we are not to listen to the voice of society that pressures us. We are not to listen to family pressure. We are not to listen to any other voice. If we are walking with our God and trusting in Him, the *only* reason we are not married is because the God of the universe, who is so good that He desires our highest welfare and who is so wise that He plans for our highest welfare and good, says no.

Knowing that God is wise totally shatters the statement one often says to himself: *I am not married because no one will have me*. There is no statement in the Word of God that states that you are not married because no one will have you. God's wisdom plans the best for you. God's power is able to execute it, and if you are trusting in God He will provide when it is best. If God leads someone to marriage, then that person's being married can bring God more glory being married than being single. Marriage is the best means to the best end that God has for that person's life. If you are single, then you can bring God more glory by being single, and singleness is the best means to the best end—God's glory and your good.

> One person wrote: The longer I know God the stronger is my confidence in His sovereign wisdom and love, and my certainty that my times are in His hands. I live with the unshakeable realization that there is nothing that can touch me, good or bad, that is not under the sovereign control of God. And this applies to my singleness, as well as to everything else.[6]

God's wisdom helps to explain those times when we pray and ask God for marriage and yet get no positive response from Him. But do you know what? The answers are often delayed. Many times God answers our prayers later that He might answer them better. His wisdom is always at work. Hannah, in 1 Samuel, was barren, and to the Hebrew mind, barrenness was the sign of God's judgment. Hannah went to the house of God and prayed often for a son. Talk about pressure! There was another woman also married to Hannah's husband, who provoked her to jealousy. The woman had borne many children, but Hannah had none. God *did* answer Hannah's prayer, but years later.

According to Luke 1, Zacharias was in the Temple offering sacrifices, and the angel came to him and said, "Do not be afraid, Zacharias, for your petition has been heard. You are going to have a son."

Zacharias was not in the Temple praying for a son. He was there performing his priestly service before God. He was not praying for a son, yet the angel told him that his prayer was heard regarding a son. What prayer? A prayer to God many years before. Verse 7 states that Elizabeth and Zacharias had no children, for Elizabeth was barren. For many years Elizabeth and Zacharias prayed and now, years later, God said, "You are going to have a son. The time is right." Maybe they lost confidence during this time, but God heard and answered. But He delayed. Why? That He might answer it better.

What if God had answered the prayer of Zacharias and Elizabeth when they first offered it? They would have had a son, but now whom do they have? They have the forerunner of Jesus Christ, John the Baptist. God was waiting for the fullness of time to come. In God's wise and unique plan, Zacharias and Elizabeth were not to have just any son, but John the Baptist. God did not answer Hannah's prayer immediately because He wanted to wait until Israel needed a godly man and leader. Then He gave Hannah Samuel.[7]

There are times when I ask God for something, and He delays. In my impatience I complain and grumble, only to see that God's delayed answer was much better than that for which I asked. Have you experienced that? How many times have we wanted something and waited and waited, only to have God answer in a manner totally different than what we expected. We could only say, ''God, I could not have done it better.''

That is what faith is all about. Even before we have that fulfillment faith says, ''God, I trust You that You are wise, and if You delay in hearing my prayer, You will delay only to answer it better in the future.'' That is faith! God always has His best for us. He does not give second best.

Because God is wise and knows what He is doing, God is not going to slight us or give us second best. He who spared not His own son, will He not give us all things freely? God sometimes delays that He might answer it better. The goodness of God desires my best and the wisdom of God plans my best.

> My Father's way may twist and turn,
> My heart may throb and ache,
> But in my soul I'm glad I know,
> He maketh no mistake.
>
> My cherished plans may go astray
> My hopes may fade away,
> But still I'll trust my Lord to lead
> For He doth know the way.
>
> Though night be dark and it may seem
> That day will never break;
> I'll pin my faith, my all in Him,
> He maketh no mistake.

There's so much now I cannot see,
My eyesight's far too dim;
But come what may, I'll simply trust
And leave it all to Him.

For by and by the mist will lift
And plain it all He'll make
Through all the way, tho' dark to me,
He made not one mistake.[8]

—Author Unknown

7

Embracing Life Fully

The Lord is trying to say something very important to those who are single. Single life does not have to be viewed as a social purgatory until one experiences the bliss of marriage. The single state does not have to be second-class or second-rate living. God wants single people to live life to the maximum, not to simply mark time until marriage. Some single people give others the impression that they are in a prison, marking time for their sentence to be carried out so that they can be released. There is no drive or life or desire to really live.

It is easy to project ourselves so much into the future that we are not able to function properly in the present. We tend to project ourselves into the future to the point that, mentally, the unfulfilled desire is fulfilled. In our minds we view ourselves as already married. If we constantly do that our emotions will become aroused, our feelings and desires will intensify, and there will be a tremendous gap between future and present realities. God wants us to live now, we need to be complete in

our singleness now. We need to become 100 percent of what
God wants us to be right now, independent of marriage. We
need to learn to embrace life fully.

We need to learn to enjoy the freedom we have as single
people. One person said:

> One of the most valuable lessons the Lord can teach us is the
> value of this moment in life, this experience. What a tendency
> we have to live in the future; "When I finish college. . . ,"
> "When I'm married. . . ," "When I get the promotion. . . ,
> "After I've been to Europe. . . ." But all we have is today,
> and it's *this* experience, *this* sunset, *this* two-day vacation, *this*
> friendship that we need to treasure. Squeeze the wine of en-
> joyment from every minute. Cultivate the beautiful quality of
> appreciation of God's gift, of others, of the intrinsic value of
> the now, however much you might stretch forward toward to-
> morrow.[1]

What opportunities we have as single people to enjoy life
right now! I am not talking about freedom to be out of God's
will and do whatever we want. It is not that kind of freedom.
Throughout the entire process of learning to enjoy life we need
to seek God's will to know what God wants us to do. We will
find that as we seek God's will, the single life can be exciting.
Think of all the things you can do as a single person. Seek
God's will regarding the development of your talents. Why just
mark time and see your talent go to waste? Develop it. God
does not hand out talents haphazardly. There is wisdom in
what He gives, and it is our privilege and our responsibility to
use it as God directs. Maybe your talent is in the area of music.
If so, develop it. If your talent is in the area of art, develop that
ability.

What about travel? A while ago I had a tremendous opportunity to travel. A friend of mine came to me and said that his boss wanted him to drive a car from Bakersfield to Boston and then pick up a car in New York City and drive it back to Bakersfield. His boss had said that he could take a friend; he gave us a credit card good for gas, lodging, and food, and $400 in traveler's checks. Away we went! We drove everywhere— Arizona, New Mexico, Dallas, Washington, D.C., West Virginia, New York City, Niagara Falls.

What about the area of writing? Maybe that is the talent, or gift, God has given you. I look back on the last few years; God has allowed me to experience one of the greatest thrills of my life—having a book published. I never dreamed of something like that's happening. It was so exciting to work on that manuscript and to have the time to be able to do that. In the next few years there are two topics I would like to develop. They may never be published, but at least I have a goal. I do not want to mark time. I want to give fully of myself to life and its opportunities.

What about education? Think about the freedom you have to go and get an education. If you want to go to a Bible school, you can go; if you want to go to seminary, you can go. Think about the opportunities that the single life offers in this area.

What about reading? Think of the last five books you have read. I am not talking about books you had to read. What about books that you have just read voluntarily, because you wanted to sit down and read them? There is an entire world of enjoyment out there in books.

One person has said:

> Much to my delight, the year after my graduation proved [to be] one of the biggest surprises of my life—it was fun! And for the following four and a half years I learned that single living is

not second-rate living. Our society is lying to us. Single living can be absolutely first-rate. It can be a short time or a life-time of learning, discovering, growing and giving.

I spent that time discovering myself. Although I thought that the self-discovery bit was complete by the time I graduated from college, I found new interests, new capabilities, new aspects of what it meant to be uniquely me. For instance, I never knew how much I'd enjoy entertaining. I found that I could cook. I could buy my own tires for my own car. And I could fill out my own income tax form. That may not sound like much, but these things added up. I could do much more than just face life. I could create it.

What a privilege it was to be single and able to dig into activities and friendships that some of my married friends had to miss. I worked in Inter-Varsity staff—one of the greatest experiences of my life. I could travel, go on vacations with friends, follow an impulse to pick up and leave town for a weekend, have friends in or stay home alone with a book. Learning to enjoy being alone, as well as being with people, was a great thing.[2]

We need to give ourselves fully to the Lord's person and to the Lord's work. There are times when my frustration over the single life is the result of a lack of concern with the things of the Lord. Whether or not I believe I have the "gift," it is critical that I apply myself to the service of Christ. To not do that is to forfeit the potential I have.

Some of you might argue that you understand, but you still want to be married. Fine. Be married in God's timing, but take advantage of the opportunities right now. A major problem is that many singles have not truly given of themselves in a devoted way to Jesus Christ and therefore are unaware of the joy that is possible in singleness.

Some single people are concerned with the things of the world when they should be concerned with the things of the Lord. If as single people our only desire is the world and securing undistracted devotion to our own desires, then we are not even in a position where God can bless us. It is obvious that frustration will result.

Since time is short we must take advantage of the opportunities given us to serve and know Christ. It may mean getting involved in a discipling ministry, or outreach ministry, or another ministry in your church. Maybe it means spending time cultivating your love walk with Jesus Christ. One person writes:

> In the area of your personal relationship with the Lord, you have a unique opportunity for closeness with Him, for developing a total trust, for leaning more completely upon His strong arm, because there is no other. Your married sister might well envy you. Somehow we've managed to make Paul's statement about the unmarrieds having more time for the Lord sound pretty dreary. That must be because we have such a dull view of God. Once our relationship has become really exciting, warm, full of love and humor (don't you ever laugh at the Lord[?]), then those remarks come alive. In the times when my soul has stood on tiptoe and I've flung my arms wide in sheer excitement over His beauty, I thought, "Don't let me lose this, Lord. If marriage would deprive me of this, forget it."[3]

8

Developing Friendships

God created us to be creatures that need each other. He made us social beings and designed that we should be part of a family—one physical, another spiritual. Look at the Trinity and you see the relationship that exists there. John 1:1 says that Jesus was "with" God, or face to face with God. The Father and Son had an intimate relationship. Therefore, when God created man it was essential that He insist that it was not good for man to be alone. God did not create man to exist as a unity. He caused a deep sleep to fall upon the man, took one of his ribs, closed up the flesh, and made a woman. As single people we must not think that the only alternative to being alone is marriage. As you look at Jesus' life, the pattern for His relationships was not marriage but friendship.[1]

Within the Trinity He had known the most perfect of friendships, and on earth He said to His disciples, in John 15:14, "You are My friends." In Luke 12:4, He said, "And I say to you, My friends . . ." Friends were important to Jesus Christ. He was motivated in His relationships by love, not by loneliness. He knew how to be alone. He did not seek relationships to escape coming to terms with Himself. He was not afraid to reach out to people and be a friend to them.

Paul's life was similar to Christ's. He traveled with Barnabas, Timothy, John Mark, Luke, and Titus. He lived for periods of time in the homes of Lydia and Priscilla and Aquila. Regardless of their age or marital status, Paul had friends. He had warm commendations for his friend Tychicus and for Onesimus, the faithful and beloved brother.

Much of the frustration single people feel is that of loneliness. When I graduated from seminary, loneliness hit me hard because school was over and the evenings became more free. Certainly, one of the greatest needs of single people is the need to love and be loved. One way that need is met is through the development of meaningful friendships. It is not good for a person to exist in isolation. We should not think that we need to wait for marriage to learn to live in intimacy with another person. Unfortunately, singles can easily equate intimacy with sexual intercourse, but should not one's definition of intimacy begin with friendship, not marriage? We know that Christ calls us to friendships right now.

Few realize the extent to which friendships can go toward meeting deep needs that we previously associated with marriage. In friendships you are supported. In friendships you are encouraged. In friendships you are able to support, give love, encourage, and accept. Friendships provide the ground for the sharing of life, which is something we all need.

> Friendship is an art that must be actively cultivated. It seldom if ever just happens. It is not enough to desire to just have friends, we must be alert, outgoing towards others, willing to give friendship, not just to receive it. True friendship costs in

time and energy and involvement and self-giving. To love a friend is to become vulnerable, to run a risk of being hurt, of suffering. There is nothing more truly worth having in this world than a Godgiven friendship.[2]

The dynamics of friendship prepare one for marriage. One lady said this:

> Friendship provides a vast scope for developing the things that are important in an individual's life: loyalty, humor, unselfishness, adjustment to another personality, companionship. A young friend writes me some telling thoughts: "Companionship is certainly available outside marriage from friendship with both sexes." If one can't handle or develop friendships of a fine quality outside marriage, how can one expect to give friendship within marriage? And many say a strong friendship is vital to a strong marriage.[3]

Friendships produce loyalty and unselfishness. Friendships force you to love. There are so many singles going around with tremendous desires for marriage but little knowledge of how to build and maintain friendships. There are some in graduate school concerning desires for marriage but in kindergarten as to how to develop a friendship. One problem that people have in a relationship with individuals of the opposite sex is that they are riding on an emotional high. Unfortunately they may make a decision to marry when on that high only to find out that disagreements do come, problems do arise. They are shocked that a relationship should have problems. They seek marriage without the dynamics of a friendship relationship; dynamics of loyalty, love, and acceptance, and communication. They enter marriage not knowing what it means to be a friend, not knowing how to love. Sometimes it is helpful to talk with people who are married to understand the dynamics of a relationship.

> No two lives, however thorough their former acquaintance may have been, however long they may have moved together in society or mingled in the closer and more intimate relations of a ripening friendship, ever find themselves perfectly in harmony on their marriage day. It is only when that mysterious blending begins after marriage which no language can explain, that each finds so much in the other that was never discovered before. There were incompatibilities that were never dreamed of until they were revealed in the attrition of domestic life.[4]

Friendships are important because friendships teach us how to love. We need to learn what it means to develop meaningful friendships. If we do that, we will become aware of two truths. First, friendships will go a long way toward meeting deep needs that we have previously associated with marriage. Second, we may find that we are not as prepared for marriage as we thought we were. Maybe God wants to teach us what it means to be a friend.

9

Living Abundantly
Through Christ

Singles must realize that marriage is not the key to fulfillment. This is a hard one, because it is so easy for us to think
that marriage is the ultimate in being fulfilled. A woman said,
"I won't be fulfilled unless I'm married. I need a man. Maybe
some women don't need a man, but I have to have one before
I'm going to be satisfied in life. I just can't live alone." Is that
the perspective God wants? Is that what He wants us to have?

The Lord Jesus Christ's statements in John 15 have been a
constant reminder to me of what my relationship with the Lord
Jesus Christ should be. In verse 1 Jesus says, "I am the true
vine." The literal translation of that is, "I am the vine, the
true one." It is interesting that Christ does not simply say, "I
am the vine." He says, "I am the *true* vine." He has something significant that He wants to emphasize by that word
"true." That word speaks of that which is genuine, trustworthy, or faithful. First Thessalonians 1:9 talks of the "true
God," in contrast to false gods. In other words, the Lord God
is genuine, or trustworthy, in contrast to gods that are *not*
trustworthy or faithful.

But there is another use of the word *true,* and it is used in this passage. It can refer to that which is eternal or that which is heavenly. It can refer to divine reality as distinguished from that which is human or earthly reality. It signifies the highest, most ultimate realization of something. For example, in John 1:9 Christ is the true light. In other words, He is the highest essence, or quality, of light in distinction from other lights, such as the stars. Christ says that He is the highest realization of what a light is. John 6:32 says that He is the true bread out of heaven. He is the perfect ideal, in contrast to physical bread. Therefore, in John 15:1 Christ is saying that He is the highest quality, the perfect ideal, the most ultimate realization of a vine.

What is a vine? The vine is the life source, the vitality. The vine yields the proper juice and nourishment to all the branches, whether small or large. All the nourishment of each branch comes from the vine. The vine is the energy, the life, the strength of the branch.

Dr. James E. Rosscup, professor at Talbot Theological Seminary, said:

> He is saying in effect, "I am the finest realization of the relationship which the Father had intended that a vine might bear to Himself. I will fulfill to the superlative degree and to the uttermost what the Father desires in a vine. I credit to myself an essence or spiritual quality that is heavenly and eternal, and not simply on the plane of earthly and temporal quality. . . . As such I am the resource beyond all resources, sufficient for the highest, deepest and most ultimate longings of man."[1]

In that statement Jesus is saying something that He wants to drive home to us. There is nothing that can give me the impetus to really live except the Lord Jesus Christ. Nothing or no one else can truly fulfill me. He alone is sufficient.

For us to really live we must allow Jesus to be our everything. Many of us suffer from the "if I only" attitude—"If I only had that job, things would be different." "If I only had that promotion . . ." "If I only had that material possesion . . ." "If I only were married . . ." Have you ever desired something, thinking that if you had it somehow your walk with the Lord would deepen, and you would be satisfied? Probably upon getting it you realized that you were still miserable and not satisfied.

We are guilty of doing the very thing that those who do not know Christ do, except we do it in reverse form. How many times have you heard people who have just come to know Christ say, "My life was really miserable before I came to know Christ. I was involved in many different things trying to find fulfillment, but then I found it in Jesus Christ. He has satisfied the longings of my heart. I have found truth. I have found life."

We start with Jesus Christ. Then what happens? We go to something else. All of a sudden Jesus Christ no longer satisfies or fulfills. We try to find fulfillment in many other things— service, ambitions, relationships. Augustine said: "Thou hast made us for Thyself, O God, and our hearts are restless until they find their rest in Thee." That is true for a nonbeliever *and* a believer. If I am restless it is probably because I am not finding my fulfillment in the person of Jesus Christ. Pascal has said that there is a God-shaped vacuum in the heart of every man which can be filled not by any created thing, but by Jesus Christ.

It is so easy to think of marriage as the ultimate in fulfillment. It is easy to think that having what we do not have would fulfill us. Even those who are married say that marriage is not the answer to fulfillment. A bride of one year wrote this to one of her girl friends:

> Your question: "Why is it that fairly often it seems like the things I'm involved in are just things to fill time until I meet the man who will cause all the regular, every day stuff to have significance?"
>
> Answer (rather, opinion): You feel that way because you're human. You're made to be hungry for a man—or something of significance that you feel like putting your time into.
>
> But even after you get a man and even get married, you'll still be hungry. Because you're human and on your way to Christlikeness, you will always have a spark of restlessness in you. I still have it, as happy and settled as I am with my husband.
>
> I still wish for something else to do, for better days, for spiritual progress in my life. That restlessness is part of being alive. Sometimes it's almost gone when you've discovered God's next step in His plan and you get all settled in a niche.
>
> But the feeling comes back and when you're single, it's easy to put your finger on the absence of a man as a cause. That may be true at that point because God is making you, or rather allowing you, to want to settle down. But that doesn't mean that when a man comes, the restlessness will go away.
>
> You'll always look ahead and want more—not in a discontented way, but in an expectant thirsty way. You'll want more of what God has, more of what He wants to teach you.
>
> When I got married, I thought I could and would put all my time into my husband and thus feel fulfilled. You know what? That never worked. Because he is a servant of the Lord, he couldn't and wouldn't want to put all his time into me. And because I was his partner, I had to put a lot of my time and

energy into his ministry, and especially into all the other people in our life together. In other words, we shared each other with everyone else.

But our time wasn't wasted when we acknowledged that it was the Lord's. It was wasted when I'd want him all to myself. When I make him my god and the center of my life, it's rotten. He hates it and I do, too. But when Christ is at the center, we're both fulfilled.[2]

True fulfillment consists of something outside ourselves. For the Christian it lies in fulfilling God's plan, not in marriage. One woman said, "I expected my husband to fulfill all my needs, and he couldn't. As a result we both felt like unfulfilled failures. Then I put my eyes on Christ, and let Him meet my need. Now, we are both satisfied."[3]

Another woman writes:

It was like a dream come true. There I was, sitting dutifully in my office, when this tall, blond, good-looking hunk walked in. He proceeded to impress me with his wit and his interest in me.

I was snowed. He took me skiing, sailing, picnicking in the mountains. We went for long walks. And he said he wanted God's will for his life. "Wow," I thought, "this is what I want." It was all too good to be true.

In fact, it was so wonderful that I wouldn't believe it at first as I had been hurt too many times before to take another chance. I prayed, "God, don't let me think this is real unless it really is."

But I finally gave in and believed that this could be it. I loved, and I even dared to think that it would work out.

Then the snow melted. He left my life as quickly as he had entered it. I was destroyed. Over the next few months my mood went from total despair to bitter resignation to grudging acceptance. I stopped talking to God—He seemed too cold and far away to listen. But finally my heart warmed up and I came around to trusting God again and believing that He loved me.

Meanwhile, this experience gave me more evidence for the case I was building. My life always seemed to revolve around a man. If I was dating someone, he filled my time and thoughts. If I had a crush on someone, I was always seeking to gain his attention. And if there was no one, which was usually the situation, I was looking for someone. Verdict: I must be made for a man.

I decided that I was meant for marriage. So I asked God, "What are You waiting for? Where is my man? Why do you always keep taking him away from me?"

I haven't been alone in these thoughts. A friend admitted, "I often feel that my time would be so much more meaningful and significant and enjoyable if there were some person into whom I could pour my life and time. I sometimes feel time is slipping away because I am without a focus, namely a man."

As I mentioned earlier, the natural desires that girls have to get married are encouraged and strengthened by almost everything we're taught. We become conditioned to believe that woman isn't complete until she's married.

One man told a 31-year-old single girl, "There must be something wrong with you, or else you're very unfeminine. Otherwise you'd be married."

Another man said to me, "Woman was made for man and isn't complete until she's married."

When I shared his comment with a close friend of mine, she replied, "If that's true, where is my man? Am I to spend half of my life, or maybe all of it, as only part of a person—incomplete?"

I agreed. When was God going to complete me?

When we cannot seem to find our fulfillment in a man, we look for it elsewhere. I sought fulfillment in my job, and it was rewarding. I looked for meaning through working with the teenagers in my church, and I really loved them. But I still felt I needed a man.

So that is what I told God. And He said, "Yes, you are meant for a man. You are meant for Me." That was startling.

Suddenly I knew that getting married was not what would fulfill me. My job wouldn't fulfill me. Helping others wouldn't do it. God Himself fulfills me—now.

The Bible tells us that the Lord has made all things for Himself (Colossians 1:1-16). Paul wrote, "And in Him [Christ] you have been made complete" (Colossians 2:10). That means whole and fulfilled.

If Christ is living in us, we are complete. He provides everything we need for living the abundant life He promises us, if we will allow Him to meet those needs. Yes, we are made for a man—we are made for God. He will bring people and things into our lives to add richness and depth. But that will not be our true source of fulfillment. It is only God who can complete and fulfill us—through Jesus Christ."[4]

Marriage is not the ultimate. Jesus Christ is the ultimate. Marriage is not the key to fulfillment. Jesus Christ is the key to fulfillment. Once we are rightly related to Him and find the source of our life in Him, then everything around us will take on greater meaning. We will never find fulfillment in an ambition, a job, or a relationship. We will find it only in Him.

NOTES

Chapter 1

1. Dan DeHaan, "The Bliss of Singleness" Before You Say I Do, cassette series, message 2. Dan DeHaan, 1610 La Vista Rd., Atlanta, GA 30329.
2. Herbert J. Miles, *Sexual Understanding Before Marriage* (Grand Rapids: Zondervan, 1972), p. 177.
3. Tumbleweeds" comic strip, *Los Angeles Times,* 21 February 1980. TUMBLEWEEDS by Tom K. Ryan. © 1980 Field Enterprises, Inc. Courtesy of Field Newspaper Syndicate.
4. Margaret Clarkson, *So You're Single* (Wheaton, Ill.: Harold Shaw, 1978), p. 30.
5. Isidor Singer, ed., *Jewish Encyclopedia,* 12 vols. (New York: Ktav, 1964), 3:636.
6. Ibid.

Chapter 2

1. John W. Fraser, trans., and David W. Torrance and Thomas F. Torrance, eds., *Calvin's New Testament Commentaries,* 12 vols. (Grand Rapids: Eerdmans, 1960), 9:135-36.
2. Richard Wurmbrand, *Tortured For Christ* (Glendale, Calif.: Diane Books, 1969), p. 36.
3. Margaret Clarkson, *So You're Single* (Wheaton, Ill.: Harold Shaw, 1978), p. 111.

Chapter 3

1. John MacArthur, "Walking in Wisdom," cassette, part 2. Grace Community Church, 13248 Roscoe Blvd., Sun Valley, CA 91352.
2. Dan DeHaan, "The Bliss of Singleness" Before You Say I Do, cassette series, message 2. Dan DeHaan, 1610 Vista Rd., Atlanta, GA 30329.
3. Ibid.

Chapter 5

1. Letha Scanzoni, *Why Wait* (Grand Rapids: Baker, 1975), p. 26.
2. Gerhard Kittel and Gerhard Friedrich, eds., 9 vols., *Theological Dictionary of the New Testament* (Grand Rapids: Eerdmans, 1964), 2:342.
3. *Universal Jewish Encyclopedia,* ed. Isaac Landman (New York: Ktav, 1969), 3:72.
4. W. Robertson Nicoll, ed., *Expositors Bible,* 25 vols. (New York: A. C. Armstrong, 1903), 19:167-68.
5. Mark W. Lee, "The Church and the Unmarried," in *It's OK to Be Single,* ed. Gary R. Collins (Waco, Tex.: Word, 1976), p. 45.
6. Ibid., p. 44.

Introduction, Part 2

1. Letha Scanzoni, *Why Wait* (Grand Rapids: Baker, 1975), p. 94.
2. Ibid., p. 96.

Chapter 6

1. Stephen Charnock, *The Existence and Attributes of God* (Grand Rapids: Sovereign Grace Publ., 1971), p. 535.
2. Elisabeth Elliot Lietsch, "Held by God's Sovereignty," *Worldwide Challenge,* January 1978, p. 40.
3. Ron Dunn, "2 Corinthians 12:1-10," cassette Campus Crusade for Christ Tape Ministries, Arrowhead Springs, San Bernardino, CA 92414.
4. Ibid.
5. J. I. Packer, *Knowing God* (Downers Grove, Ill: Inter-Varsity, 1973), p. 80.
6. Margaret Clarkson, *So You're Single* (Wheaton, Ill.: Harold Shaw, 1978), p. 32.
7. Ron Dunn, "If God Doesn't Answer," [James 4:1-3], cassette. Lifestyle Ministries, Inc., P.O. Box 3087, Irving, TX 75061.

Chapter 7

1. Gini Andrews, *Your Half of the Apple* (Grand Rapids: Zondervan, 1972), pp. 66-67.
2. Alice Fryling, "The Grace of Single Living," in C. Stephen Board, *His Guide to Sex, Singleness and Marriage* (Downers Grove, Ill.: Inter-Varsity, 1974), pp. 74-75.
3. Andrews, p. 67.

Chapter 8

1. Nancy Hardesty, "Being Single in Today's Word," in *It's OK to Be Single,* p. 11.
2. Margaret Clarkson, *So You're Single* (Wheaton, Ill.: Harold Shaw, 1978), p. 75.
3. Gini Andrews, *Your Half of the Apple* (Grand Rapids: Zondervan, 1972), p. 67.
4. Cited in Paul E. Billheimer, *Don't Waste Your Sorrows* (Fort Washington, Pa.: Christian Literature Crusade, 1977), p. 88.

Chapter 9

1. James E. Rosscup, *Abiding in Christ* (Grand Rapids: Zondervan, 1973), p. 31.
2. Judy Downs Douglass, *Old Maid Is a Dirty Word* (San Bernardino, Calif.: Campus Crusade for Christ, 1977), pp. 54-56.
3. Ibid., p. 59.
4. Ibid., pp. 35-37.